# Maison d'Artiste
# Unfinished De Stijl Icon

‘He wants … to build a model house in the country with the help of the De Stijl artists.’

Letter from Theo van Doesburg to J.J.P. Oud about
Léonce Rosenberg’s plans, 19 October 1920.

‘In a joint study we proceeded on the basis of an architecture representing the unity of all the arts, industry, engineering, etc., and have determined that the result of this will be a new style.’

Translation of statement 1 from the manifesto by
Theo van Doesburg, Cornelis van Eesteren and Gerrit Rietveld,
‘Vers une Construction Collective’, 1923

‘In the last design (house of an artist) the greatest effort was made to meet all domestic functions and needs in the freest possible connection.’

Explanation by Cornelis van Eesteren of Maison d’Artiste, c. 1925-1931

# Maison d'Artiste.

## Unfinished De Stijl Icon

Dolf Broekhuizen (ed.)

nai010 publishers

# Contents



---

# Foreword

During the past ten years I have carried out a number of commissions in Paris and elsewhere in France and what struck me on each occasion was that I was able to build on the very strong reputation enjoyed by Dutch architecture – a reputation built by previous generations. Within the French professional world the name Theo van Doesburg still resonates. I had come into contact with his work during my training as architect–urban designer. Van Doesburg's prodigious creativity and ever-inquiring mind and his practice of applying a free imagination to the spatial exploration of designing remain for many today an enduring inspiration. Looking at Van Doesburg's work one also becomes increasingly aware of the extent to which architecture can be enriched by maintaining close ties with the art world and other disciplines.

Recognition of Van Doesburg's importance in international art and architectural history is not confined to a small band of connoisseurs, either. He played an indelible role in the development of the Bauhaus and as the founder of De Stijl – two art and architectural movements that are known and esteemed worldwide.

Anyone who studies Van Doesburg's work finds themselves in a kaleidoscopic world the fascinates with its combination of absolute clarity and profundity. The intellectual and artistic breadth that characterizes his person and his life is as impressive as it is enviable. He was part of a network of leading artists, designers and architects in a period that was both exciting and turbulent: the first three decades of the twentieth century. From 1912, Van Doesburg, having started out as an artist, wrote reviews and art criticism, first on visual art, but before long on every facet of culture, including music, design and composition. In the process he expanded his expertise via the work of a select array of avant-gardists, incorporating what he had learned from them into his own work. He designed superb stained-glass windows for, among others, a social housing complex in Rotterdam.

His stay in Weimar, the city of Bauhaus, turned him even more decidedly in the direction of architecture. He had arrived there in 1921 at the end of his European lecture tour on De Stijl. There he met the young architect Cornelis van Eesteren, who was travelling around Europe on a Prix de Rome scholarship. The younger man was impressed by Van Doesburg's ideas and thus began a short but momentous collaboration. Together, Van Doesburg and Van Eesteren designed a studio house, Maison d'Artiste, as well as two other houses. The Maison d'Artiste in particular is still of interest to the current design culture because it is such a compelling demonstration of the innovative character of their fundamental, design-led research. It shows how such exploratory design can open up new avenues. Although the house was not realized at the time, its design and that of the Maison Particulière have played a crucial role the development of architecture and culture, thanks to the wealth of ideas embodied in the two designs. It is telling that the photo in which the two men are seen working on a model has acquired iconic status.

As Chief Government Architect, it is my ambition in the coming years to broaden thinking within architecture and in so doing promote the position of innovative design. I want to encourage architects to bring their creativity to bear on the design process, in order to formulate fundamentally new solutions for all the new technological and social issues confronting our generation. Here, too, the life and work of Theo van Doesburg can serve as inspiration.

De Stijl was recently included in the Canon of Dutch History. If the Maison d'Artiste were to be realized, it would be possible to physically experience this icon of Dutch culture on a true scale for the first time, rendering a historical phenomenon from 1923 tangible in all its force.

This publication is aimed at bringing that realization a step closer, in the knowledge that it is no easy task to make the original design fully buildable. In addition, the heirs of Van Doesburg and Van Eesteren own the copyright on the design and their views must also be taken into account. One of the parties involved argues in this book that by taking design decisions step-by-step, incrementally, the decision-making process can be steered in the right direction. Various disciplines can be enlisted for this task and designers could make use of their knowledge of new construction methods and scientific research in order to turn the historical design into a realizable building that in every respect fulfils the original ambitions and dreams of its creators.

It is marvellous to see that the strength of their idea, translated into an intriguing design, has effortlessly survived for almost one hundred years without losing either its brilliance or its modernity. I sincerely hope that this publication and the depiction of potential realizations will succeed in stimulating clients and sponsors to actually want to build the Maison d'Artiste.

Floris Alkemade,
Chief Government Architect

1 Theo van Doesburg and Cornelis van Eesteren, Maison d'Artiste, 1923, photo of model, entrance side. Maison d'Artiste developed into an icon of De Stijl
Het Nieuwe Instituut, Rotterdam

Dolf Broekhuizen

# Introduction

## Maison d'Artiste: an unfinished icon

They were so incredibly proud. And exhausted. When the design for an artist's residence, 'Maison d'Artiste', went on show in October 1923, the presentation material had only just been finished. Together, the artist Theo van Doesburg (1883–1931) and the architect Cornelis van Eesteren (1897–1988) had spent the months leading up to the opening working feverishly on the De Stijl exhibition, of which this design was one of the key works. Night after long night they had worked on the drawings and the model. The Maison d'Artiste was intended to show just how innovative De Stijl was. In Van Doesburg's view the De Stijl group was, in the Netherlands at least, the most important avant-garde movement and right then it was a trendsetter as well. The model was more than a purely spatial sculpture; it could also be regarded as a manifesto for a new architecture. With it they would set their stamp on the art world. For Van Doesburg, the exhibition 'Les Architectes du Groupe "de Styl"', in the gallery of the respected art dealer Léonce Rosenberg (1879–1947) in the heart of the art world, Paris, was proof that De Stijl was receiving international recognition and was more than the magazine for which he was the tireless propagandist.

The Maison d'Artiste is one of three designs the two Dutch designers made specifically for the Paris exhibition [fig. 1]. What is special about this design and the other two, 'Maison Particulière', a private residence and 'Maison Rosenberg' (also known as Hôtel Particulier), a house with museum for the Rosenburg art collection, is that they were based on a new conception of architecture and living. And of the three, Maison d'Artiste was its most radical expression. The Maison Particulière and the Maison Rosenberg were composed of volumes and planes slotted into one another as independent elements, which then made up a single whole [figs. 2, 3]. The Maison d'Artiste is more radical, because here the rooms are placed on different levels in discrete volumes that appear almost to float. The system of load-bearing walls is completely abandoned. Instead of a corridor, a staircase functions as the central core, binding the various rooms together and providing a dynamic spatial experience. Because rooms spill over into one another, a freer manner of living is possible. While the windows in the Maison Particulière were still designed as a hole in the wall, as was customary at that time, in Maison d'Artiste Van Doesburg and Van Eesteren went a step further and windows span the facade or even occupy an entire wall. Colour planes and facade planes are congruent, which serves to emphasize the basic constituents of architecture, such as space, surface and colour, and gives the architecture a new aesthetic. Indeed, painting and architecture coincide totally, forming a harmonious whole that offers the occupant powerful impressions, rendering the separate disciplines of painting and sculpture redundant.

One can only imagine the disappointment Van Doesburg must have felt a few years later when he discovered that, after the exhibition, his models had ended up in the cellar of the publisher of the avant-garde magazine, *L'Architecture vivante*, where they had succumbed to the damp. All that remained were the design drawings and a few black-and-white photographs of the models. The project remained forever in the design phase and was never realized. The discrepancies between the drawings and the model of the Maison d'Artiste reveal that the designers were still feeling their way, that it was a 'work in progress'. Anyone wanting to realize the house, will need to take new decisions in order to convert the design into a realizable plan.

Although the Maison d'Artiste did not progress beyond a design, it was nevertheless not without influence. Since that 1923 exhibition, Van Doesburg and Van Eesteren's projects have secured a special place in the development of modern architecture and visual art. The Maison d'Artiste belongs to the Dutch cultural canon. De Stijl is without doubt one of the most important Dutch contributions to early twentieth-century cultural

2 Theo van Doesburg and Cornelis van Eesteren, counter-construction Maison Particulière, 1923, gouache on collotype
Het Nieuwe Instituut, Rotterdam

expression (design, architecture, art, literature, music), even though there is still debate about what exactly De Stijl was – as magazine, movement or idea. The Maison d'Artiste and the Maison Particulière and the equally famous 'counter-constructions', the axonometric projections in which the floor and facade planes of structures are rendered in an almost dizzying perspective and architecture is transformed into an almost abstract spatial sculpture, have become icons of De Stijl architecture [fig. 2]. Major architecture and art museums, like Het Nieuwe Instituut in Rotterdam and the Museum of Modern Art in New York, have included the original drawings, photographs or collotypes of the design in their collection.

## De Stijl one hundred years on

In 2017 it will be one hundred years since the publication of the first issue of the magazine *De Stijl*, with which, indirectly, Van Doesburg also launched the movement. Several Dutch museums will be celebrating the anniversary with research projects and exhibitions. This publication aims to reveal the cultural-historical significance of the Maison d'Artiste and at the same time to elucidate themes relating to the posthumous realization of the design.

The Maison d'Artiste's exemplary function as a manifesto of De Stijl justifies the key question, namely, what possibilities and dilemmas would arise if the design were finally to be built? In various chapters the most important possibilities are considered and comparisons are drawn with reconstructions and 'late realizations' (executions of designs long after the architect has died) of other designs. In a full-scale realization of the Maison d'Artiste there would be no question of a reconstruction or a restoration, because no full-size version ever existed. Construction from scratch would be based on an interpretation and translation of the original design. Every realization creates a new situation whose objective is not historically determined, but is established in the present day. Architect and client would need to make judgements and adopt fundamental positions. If you are set on rendering visible the 'essence of the design', you first need to decide what that essence is. If the objective is 'spatial experience', then the new interior will be subordinate to the original spatial concepts. Or perhaps it is all a matter of a 'historical sensation', where people are given the opportunity to experience the world of 1923. Finding answers to such questions entails careful assessments and cultural choices, which are inextricably bound up with the chosen or desired function.

It is fascinating to imagine that it might yet be possible to experience the Maison d'Artiste. Because the qualities of the design are closely linked to the design decisions, the interpretations and original intentions of Van Eesteren and Van Doesburg are given due attention in this book. Existing, often excellent, studies served as a starting point, because De Stijl artists and designers like Van Doesburg, Van Eesteren, Rietveld and Mondrian have received ample attention since the 1950s in art-historical research and museum survey exhibitions. In addition, the authors of this publication place the Maison d'Artiste in new contexts coupled to new perceptions and insights.

## Organization of the book

*Maison d'Artiste. Unfinished De Stijl Icon* consists of three parts. In the first of these the authors examine the broader cultural-historical significance of the Maison d'Artiste. Michael White, Professor in History of Art, identifies the model's dual function: as a model for a building yet to be realized and as an expression of an idea about architecture. Architectural historian Dolf Broekhuizen discusses the hypothesis that the Maison d'Artiste was intended to be a model home. He draws comparisons with full-scale prototypes built for housing expos within the framework of museum presentations and open-air exhibitions.

The second part focuses on the designers' intentions and places them in the context of the historical avant-garde. Art historian Alied Ottevanger analyses Van Doesburg's ideas as articulated in his correspondence and articles. She looks at what preceded the models: Van Doesburg's pursuit of a monumental art and international promotion. Architecture historian Kees Somer examines in his contribution the ideas of the co-designer of the Maison d'Artiste, Cornelis van Eesteren, finding a connection between 'Collective Construction' and the theoretical publications of developmental psychology. Dolf Broekhuizen focuses on the reception accorded the Maison d'Artiste and De Stijl, referring to a number of contemporaries, such as Mondrian and Rietveld, as well as critics and later historians who have written about their significance and underlying ideas. In this context he presents a new source which served as starting point for the 'basic elements' on which Van Doesburg's theory for Maison d'Artiste was based. The picture section, the heart of the book, documents the three Paris models: Maison d'Artiste, Maison Particulière and Maison Rosenberg. This documentation, which enhances the book's value as a reference work, forms the lead-in to the third and final part, which examines the possibilities and dilemmas of realization. Every realization is an interpretation. Dolf Broekhuizen details the attempts that have been made to realize the design to date and the dilemmas that arose. He presents new insights regarding the building materials for the Maison d'Artiste. Public administration expert Wouter Jan Verheul writes about the embedding of significant buildings in their location. What are the factors determining success or failure? The final chapter looks at international examples of buildings constructed after the death of the architect. The case studies highlighted by Professor of Heritage and Cultural Value Paul Meurs reveal various options with respect to authenticity and the possibility of several chronological layers. In the afterword, cultural and architectural historian Ole Bouman gives his views on the importance of the Maison d'Artiste for today's culture, relating the significance of possible realization to the historiography of De Stijl.

This wide-ranging picture of the Maison d'Artiste contributes not only to the historiography of De Stijl, but also to the current debate about architecture and urban design, in which the way we deal with history, existing buildings and historical heritage is more relevant than ever for a meaningful built environment.

3 Theo van Doesburg and Cornelis van Eesteren, Maison Rosenberg (Hôtel Particulier), 1923, photo of model, garden side
Het Nieuwe Instituut, Rotterdam

4 General view of the 'Les Architectes du Groupe "De Styl"' exhibition, in the L'Effort Moderne gallery, Paris, 15 October to 15 November 1923.
Right in the middle on the table, Maison Rosenberg; in the corner against the wall right, Maison d'Artiste; Maison Particulière in the room left; and the public transport shelter by Willem van Leusden between two passageways.
Het Nieuwe Instituut, Rotterdam

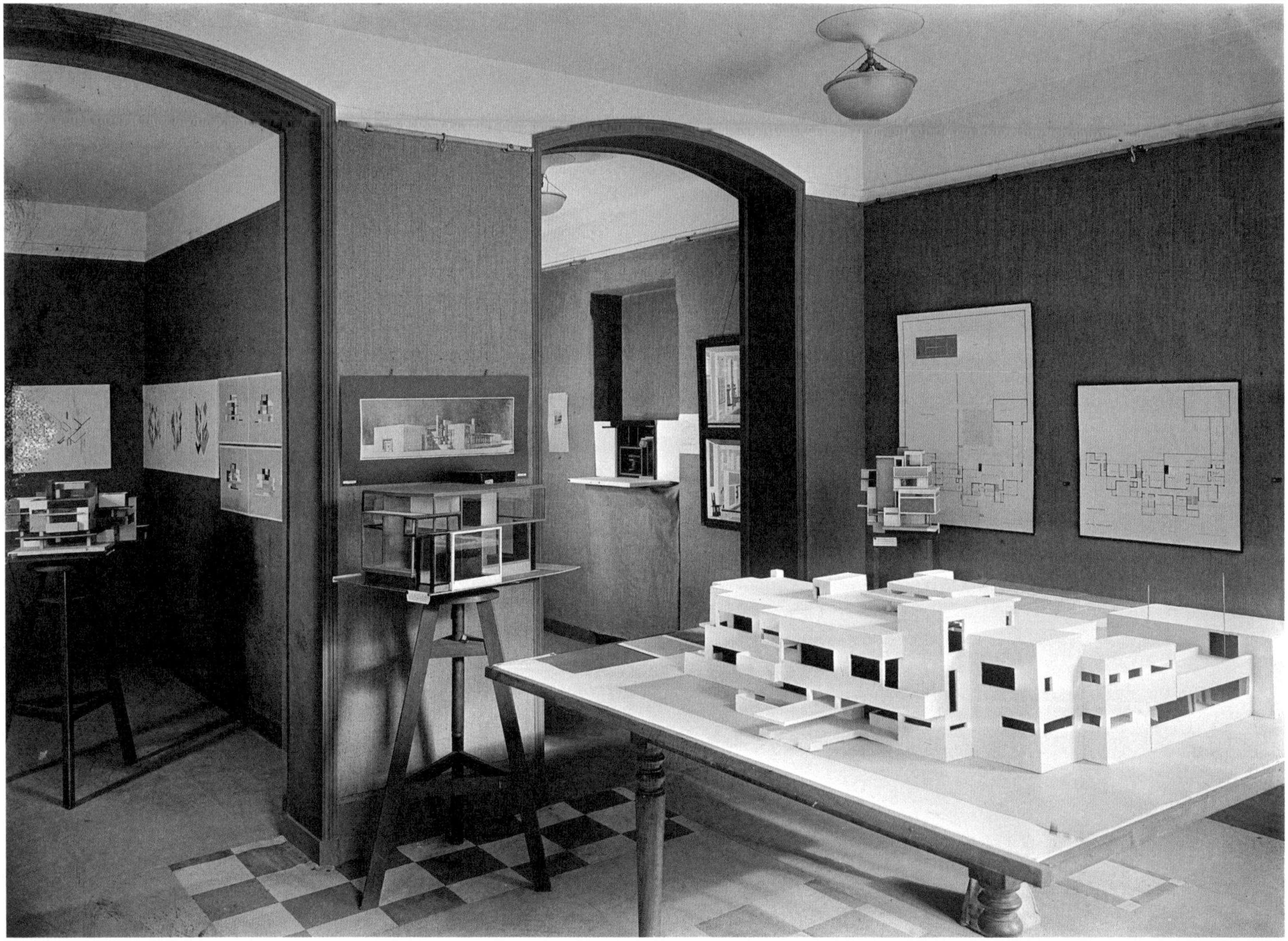

Michael White

# Model Living
# The Maison d'Artiste as representation and idea

### 'What do you think of that English futuristic "Home"?'

In late 1919 the British artist, Wyndham Lewis (1882-1957), sent Theo van Doesburg a copy of his latest publication together with a number of issues of the national newspaper, the *Daily Mirror*. Van Doesburg sketched the front page of one of these in a letter to J.J.P.Oud, asking him, 'What do you think of that English futuristic "Home"?' [figs. 5, 6].[1] The page in question was dominated by a photograph of a model, titled 'A suggestion for a building', made by the painter Edward Wadsworth (1889-1949), currently on display in a London exhibition [fig. 7].[2] 'It is enough to make Wren ... turn in his grave,' complained the paper and compared the model unfavourably to another that 'more closely resembles a modern building than the jigsaw puzzle seen above.'[3]

Disregarding the negative commentary, Van Doesburg was clearly impressed by the outlandishness of the model and eagerly imagined this as a means to get publicity for De Stijl. He drew for Oud two related imaginary front pages of newspapers featuring De Stijl in the form of painting and architecture, represented by works by Piet Mondrian (1872-1944) and Oud (1890-1963) respectively. Van Doesburg's placement of the image of Wadsworth's model between a sketch of a recent diamond-shaped painting by Mondrian and Oud's design for a factory in Purmerend reflects his ambition for De Stijl to synthesize painting and architecture. It also looks ahead to his own architectural models made for the 1923 exhibition 'Les Architectes du Groupe "De Styl"' with their integration of functional and aesthetic elements.[4] What has yet to be fully appreciated, though, is how, of these, the model of the Maison d'Artiste in particular was conceived by Van Doesburg to be both a representation of a building, one that might at some point be realizable, and a proposition, a 'suggestion' (to use Wadsworth's term), an idea about architecture, with the ultimate realization of a building of less importance than the experience it offered in itself. It is that dual aspect of the model, its role both as a maquette (a small-scale version of an object from which a larger one can be constructed) and as a concept that will be the concern of this essay.

### A proposal for a way of life yet to come

Just after the opening of 'Les Architectes du Groupe "De Styl"' at the gallery L'Effort Moderne, Van Doesburg wrote to his friend, Antony Kok (1882-1969), to give a fulsome description of the exhibition. Clearly delighted, he rattled off a list of what was on display, starting, naturally, with the main item that dominated Room 1, the grand model of a Hôtel Particulier intended for Léonce Rosenberg, the owner of L'Effort Moderne, designed as a country house with gallery attached. However, Van Doesburg's account of it was purely matter-of-fact; he commented only on how large it was, and also on its late arrival, meaning that there was no time to give it colour. He was much more excited by another object in the room, one that had also only just been finished, 'a model of an ideal little house all in colour.'[5] In the installation photograph, we can see this 'little house', the Maison d'Artiste, in the right-hand corner, squeezed in so that it actually obscured part of the ground floor plan of the Hôtel Particulier on the wall behind [fig. 4]. Its position makes it look like a late arrival, as if there was nowhere else to put it.

1 'Wat zeg je van dat engelsche futuristische "Home"?' Theo van Doesburg, letter to J.J.P. Oud, [30?] November 1919. RKD, VDA, cat. no. 149. From the letter is deducible that the publication Lewis sent was W. Lewis, *The Caliph's Design: Architects! Where is Your Vortex?*, London: The Egoist Ltd., 1919.

2 Arts League Service 1919.

3 Refers to the architect and scientist Christopher Wren (1632-1723); Anonymous 1919.

4 'Les Architectes du Groupe "De Styl"', L'Effort Moderne, Paris, 15 October to 15 November 1923. The exhibition had originated in the design of a country house with art gallery for Léonce Rosenberg, the owner of the gallery in which it took place. See the contribution by Alied Ottevanger in this book.

5 Theo van Doesburg, letter to Antony Kok, 18 October 1923. Quoted in: Ottevanger 2008, p. 439.

Of the three models in the exhibition on which Van Doesburg collaborated, the Maison d'Artiste was the one for which he was most responsible.[6] His eagerness to highlight it both in the exhibition and in his description to Kok is therefore obvious. Furthermore, unlike the Hôtel Particulier, he had not been constrained by a client's requirements and could let his imagination run free. According to two art historians, Nancy Troy and Evert van Straaten, the Maison d'Artiste would have been impossible

Mondrian had declined to take part in the exhibition because he thought it *te vroeg* ('too early') for the presentation of something such as De Stijl architecture.[9] We might recall that it was the newspaper that had called Wadsworth's model a 'home' in order to make it appear even more alien, to emphasize its unhomeliness and provoke a negative response from its readers. But that is just what caught Van Doesburg's eye. He was attracted by its rejection of anything obviously comfortable and cosy.

5 Letter from Theo van Doesburg to J.J.P. Oud, November 1919. Excerpt from a letter with drawings by Van Doesburg for a front page.
RKD – Netherlands Institute for Art History, The Hague

PREMIER: BANKRUPTCY, WAY TO BOLSHEVISM

The Daily Mirror

V.C.'s WIDOW RE-WEDS

A FUTURIST'S IDEA OF A HOME.

GENERALS CRITICISED IN DARDANELLES REPORT.

6 Edward Wadsworth's 'suggestion for a building' and E. McKnight Kauffer's 'idea of a model public-house' at the Exhibition of Practical Arts. Cover of *The Daily Mirror*, 18 November 1919

to build at the time.[7] Jean Leering emphasized the aesthetic qualities of the Maison d'Artiste and how it resolved the colour construction problems presented in the axonometric drawings of the Maison Particulière, the third model that Van Doesburg collaborated on in the exhibition with the young architect Cornelis van Eesteren: 'The colour planes and the composition of the facade surfaces are in total harmony.'[8] In the same way that Van Doesburg interpreted Wadsworth's model not just as Futurist but as futuristic, Van Doesburg's *ideal huisje* ('ideal little house') has predominantly been presented as *ideaal* in the sense of its being unrealizable, not of the present, a proposal for a way of life yet to come.

The ambition was to transform life, just as, when Mondrian wrote about Neoplasticism and architecture in 1926, he specifically stated that 'The idea of the "home" – "Home, Sweet Home" – must be destroyed.'[10]

Nevertheless, it has also not gone without mention that the concept of the Maison d'Artiste suited Van Doesburg's current personal situation very well.[11] A studio house with a music room was exactly what he would have longed for at that moment, for himself and for his wife Nelly van Doesburg, who was a pianist. At the time of the exhibition, they were both camping out at Mondrian's and did not have a fixed address of their own until February 1924. Van Doesburg's term *ideaal* might have had a much more practical sense, meaning 'just right'. It is time, therefore, to look a bit harder at how the Maison d'Artiste was not just beyond its time but also very much of its time.

## Van Doesburg and modern living

Van Doesburg's previous mention of the Maison d'Artiste (again in a letter to Kok) described it slightly differently: 'I've also designed a very modern house.'[12] We can readily identify 'modern' aspects to the house that are not just to do with its extraordinary appearance. For example (as was the case also with the Maison Particulière), the design does not specify a separate dining and reception room on the ground floor but a less specific *salle commune*, which could potentially be used for a variety of functions [fig. 8]. Glazed on two sides, this room is presented as extremely public, directly accessible and highly visible from the entrance (ground floor). The studio and music rooms dominate the design in terms of their size in relation to the overall plan, emphasizing the house as a place of activity rather than refuge (first floor). The comparatively large amount of space given to the *chambre d'amis* again draws attention to sociability and interaction, rather than privacy and family life (second floor). At the top of the building was a *salle de culture physique* (third floor). Light, air and bodily movement, all concerns of 'modern' architecture of the time, are figured in the many terraces projecting at all levels and on all sides of the building.

A FUTURIST'S IDEA OF A HOME.

"A suggestion for a building" is the catalogue description of this Futurist "model," shown by Mr. Edward Wadsworth at the Exhibition of Practical Arts now being held by the Arts' League Service at Durham House-street, Adelphi. It is enough to make Wren, who did so much to beautify London, turn in his grave. The builder is supposed to find places for the windows from the "plan."

7 Edward Wadsworth's 'suggestion for a building', *The Daily Mirror*, 18 November 1919

Although of much smaller dimensions than either the Hôtel Particulier or the Maison Particulière, the Maison d'Artiste retained a *chambre de domestique*, but unlike the other two designs, did not create a separate circulation route for service. The large staircase, glazed on two sides, is the only route up and down the building for all occupants, and all rooms are arranged in direct relation to it, removing the need for corridors. Furthermore, the distribution of rooms in direct relation to the staircase permitted greater flexibility across storeys. In the Maison Particulière all bedrooms were designed to be on the same level. The Maison d'Artiste has a much less clear division; an incremental stepping-up around the staircase can be read most clearly in the spiral staggering of the *chambre de domestique*, the *chambre d'amis* and the main *chambre à coucher*. Despite the residual hierarchy this implies, the modernity of the Maison d'Artiste can in fact be found in its expression of fluid social relationships, of permeability, and need for mobile, active inhabitants. The glass staircase acts as a vertical corridor, one in which all the movements of occupants are visible.

**6** The history of the collaboration between Theo van Doesburg and Cornelis van Eesteren on the models of the Hôtel Particulier, Maison Particulière and Maison d'Artiste is too complex to cover here. See the discussion in Hoek 2000, pp. 343-345.

**7** Troy 1983, p. 112; Van Straaten, 1988, p. 142.

**8** Leering 1968, p. 22 .

**9** Theo van Doesburg, letter to Antony Kok, undated [last week of July 1923]. Quoted in Ottevanger 2008, p. 430.

**10** Mondrian 1927, p. 18. Based on the translation in Holtzman and James 1993 p. 211.

**11** Van Straaten 1988, p. 139.

**12** Theo van Doesburg letter to Antony Kok, 6 August 1923. Quoted in Ottevanger 2008, p. 436.

8 Theo van Doesburg and Cornelis van Eesteren, *Maison d'Artiste*, floor plans, 1923.
Top left 'ground floor', top right 'first floor', bottom right 'second floor', bottom left 'third floor'
RKD – Netherlands Institute for Art History, The Hague,

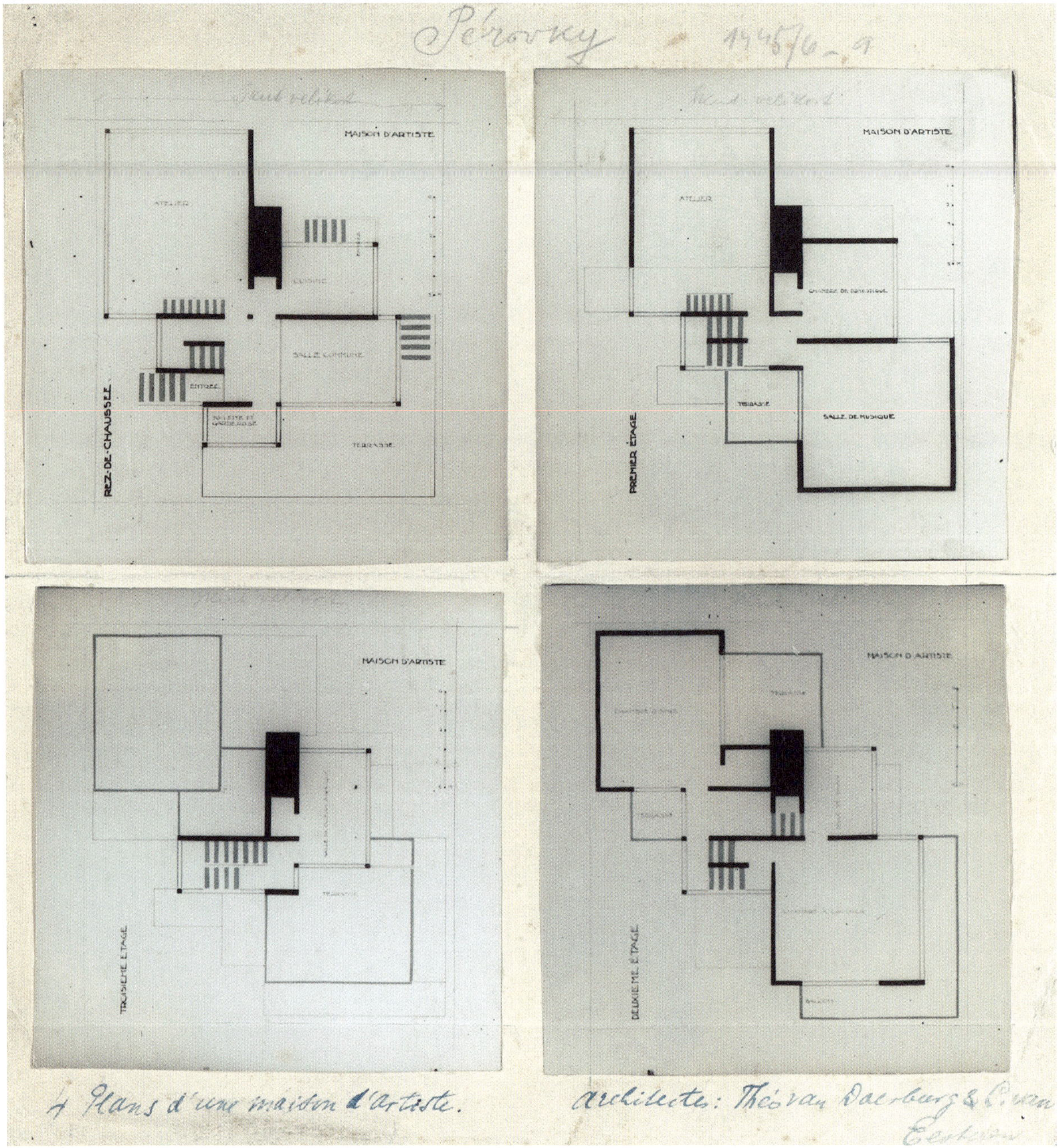

Van Doesburg's collaborator, Cornelis van Eesteren, writing a few years after the event, emphasized the key modern features of the Maison d'Artiste to be its 'free floor plan, i.e. a functional floor plan in which e.g. the windows are placed just where people need light or can take advantage of a view and which gives the rooms the form [they] need in connection with their purpose.' Where, initially, the Maison d'Artiste appears rather fantastical, Van Eesteren saw its design driven by concern for function: 'The kitchen is for cooking etc. The living room for getting together and shared activities, study for working. On the one hand a separation of rooms based on use, on the other hand an easy transition from one to the other.'[13] Mobility was also a key factor for him: 'One could talk about activating dwellings with possibilities everywhere for genuine rest and relaxation.'[14]

While seemingly an exceptional building for an exceptional occupant, the Maison d'Artiste was responding to the changing nature of the home, as it became ever penetrated by the forces of leisure and technology. The press had been primed to perceive Wadsworth's 'suggestion for a building' as a house by the successive Ideal Home Exhibitions that had been initiated a decade or so earlier, where labour-saving domestic appliances were displayed alongside proposals by both architects and members of the public for 'dream' homes.[15] In 1920, the Ideal Home Exhibition featured an 'all-electric' house, for example. Oud, who was in Britain researching system-building techniques, visited it.[16] However, it was not until a few years later, in a review of a different type of exhibition, that Van Doesburg made comments that can help us fully to see what connects the Maison d'Artiste to current debates about modern living.

## The ultimate surface

Describing the 1927 Deutsche Werkbund exhibition, 'Die Wohnung', in Stuttgart (often known as the *Weissenhofsiedlung*), Van Doesburg made a number of remarkable statements, not least that 'Houses are like people. Their features, posture, gait, clothing, in short: their surface, is a reflection of their thinking, their inner life.'[17] The anthropomorphism of the first sentence is in striking contrast to the anti-mimetic, abstract aesthetic of De Stijl, which did away with obvious bodily representation by rejecting such features as figuration in painting and symmetry in architecture. Van Doesburg balanced his emphasis on external appearance, though, by his reference to the 'inner life' at the end of the next sentence, which seems more in keeping with the philosophical ambitions of De Stijl. The decisive term that links the two, external appearance and internal life, is surface. Elsewhere in his review Van Doesburg stated dramatically that 'only the *ultimate surface* is decisive in architecture', and that 'only the surface is of importance for people. Man does not live within the construction, within the architectural skeleton, but only touches architecture essentially through its ultimate surface.'[18]

The discourse of architectural surface that Van Doesburg articulated so powerfully in 1927 had been present in De Stijl from its beginning and was most frequently accompanied by the analogy of clothing. It was Oud who introduced this approach. He had used it as early as 1913, in a critique of the persistence of traditional Dutch architectural styles, which he compared to the ludicrous image of someone appearing on the streets of the Amsterdam wearing 'the "traditional" Marken knickerbockers'.[19] By the time of Van Doesburg's letter, asking for his opinion on Wadsworth's 'futuristic "Home"', the connection between fashion and architecture had become fully integrated in Oud's writings.[20] He had inherited this approach from his architectural mentor, H.P. Berlage, who, for example, in his important essay 'Beschouwingen over stijl' (Thoughts on Style, 1922) made the idea of clothing central to the problem of contemporary architecture: 'The architecture was a tastelessly clad person.'[21] Berlage, in turn, had taken the idea of architecture as the clothing of space from the German theorist Gottfried Semper, who had articulated his *Prinzip der Bekleidung* in his major tome of 1860, *Der Stil*. Just as Van Doesburg described surface as

**13** Written by Van Eesteren between 1925 and 1931 in relation to Maison particulière and Maison d'Artiste. According to Van Eesteren this aspect was most evident in Maison d'Artiste, HNI, EEST, 3.358.1, Van Eesteren 1931; Bock 2001, p. 131.
**14** Van Eesteren 1931. Quoted in Bock 2001, pp. 131-132.
**15** It is worth noting that the origins of the Vorticist movement, of which Wadsworth was a member, go back to the fall-out from a commission for the Omega Workshops to decorate a room for the 1913 Ideal Home Exhibition. Edwards 2000, p. 12.
**16** Langmead 1999, p. 35.
**17** Theo van Doesburg, 'Stuttgart-Weißenhof 1927: Die Wohnung'. Based on the Dutch translation in: Boekraad (ed.) 1986, p. 169.
**18** Theo van Doesburg, 'Stuttgart-Weißenhof 1927: Die Wohnung'. Based on the Dutch translation in: Boekraad (ed.) 1986, p. 169.
**19** J.J.P.Oud 1913, p. 223.
**20** Significant examples are Oud 1919 and Oud 1921.
**21** Berlage 1922, p. 72.

all important, Semper had explained the origin of architecture not in structure but in its covering.[22]

Van Doesburg extended his anthropomorphic account of architecture in 1927 to suggest that 'everyone carries his surroundings, his atmosphere with him', a statement that can be amusingly compared to a drawing he published in his Dadaist journal *Mécano* in 1922 of 'the confrontation of the natural and mechanical men in Weimar in 1922' [fig. 9], which features an abstract-looking figure almost certainly intended to represent Van Doesburg himself. The figure takes the form of a straight black line, extending into a top hat, and merges with a square and various floating points of intersection behind it, close to a caricature of Van Doesburg's statement that 'houses are like people'. In Weimar, Van Doesburg had purchased new clothes in order to appear, as he put it in a letter to Oud, 'as taut as possible' continuing that, 'having identified this clothing as modern I've carried it through to the utmost perfection. Modern clothing is first and foremost sports clothing: life is a sport and the clothing must bear witness to the electric atmosphere of large centres of activity.'[23]

Banal though a direct comparison between Van Doesburg's wardrobe and his architecture certainly is, it does help us to see how contemporary male clothing could be seen by the likes of Van Doesburg, Oud and others as on the one hand analogous to the elimination of individuality, while on the other essential to the liberation of the individual from the burdens of uniformity. As Mondrian was keen to point out, 'taut modern clothing' was not the same as 'natural clothing' or even 'nakedness'.[24] If, on the face of it, surface in architecture, as theorized by Van Doesburg, suggested something sheer, unmodulated and unornamented, it was not to be confused with blankness or absence. A large amount of his 1927 review is given over to a discussion of glass and how its presentation could bring out 'the maximum energy force of the material itself'.[25]

## Semi-opacity and surface

In its corner location in the exhibition, the model of the Maison d'Artiste could only be seen from one aspect. The angle visitors were given emphasized the model's full-height glazed staircase, a deliberate decision, no doubt, to contrast its verticality to the horizontal, spreading Hôtel Particulier, the plain whiteness of the latter also compensated for by what Van Doesburg assured Kok were the 'marvellous' colours of the former.[26] However, if we look closely and compare the model to the third one in the room to the left (which is a model of Willem van Leusden's design for a public transport shelter), we can see that Van Doesburg must have done something to the glazing of the staircase to make it semi-opaque, seemingly diminishing one of its key features.[27] The manner in which the glass reflects the surfaces next to it in photographs of the model tells us how its material qualities were transformed by this choice. In the two coloured drawings of the

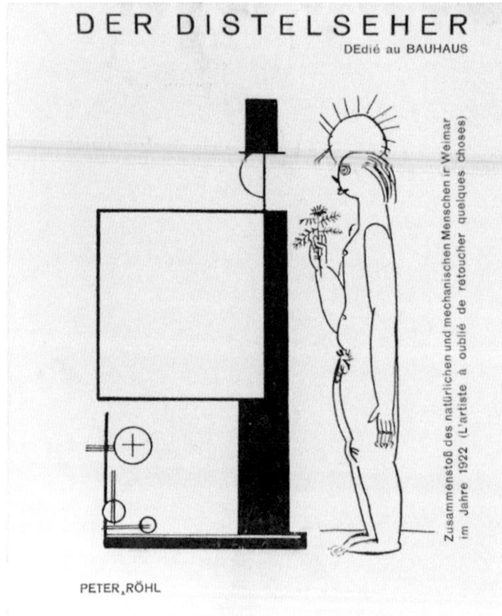


9 Peter Röhl, 'Der Distelseher', in: *Mécano*, no. *Blue, Blauw. Blau, Blue*, 1922. Figure left: possibly Theo van Doesburg. Figure right: possibly Bauhaus teacher Johannes Itten

Maison d'Artiste, we can see this area has been painted white. On one drawing of the elevation Van Doesburg wrote the word *witglas* (white glass) to differentiate it from ordinary *glas* for the other windows.[28] In his commentary on the exhibition to Kok, Van Doesburg described the materials he used for the model as copper, wood, mica, cardboard and glass. Mica is a silicate that was used in sheet form for small windows in boilers, lanterns and stoves because of its resistance to high temperatures. To glaze the staircase at full-scale Van Doesburg may have had in mind the white 'Gisoglas' that Willem Gispen had devised for his range of light fixtures and lamps, which was a material available in relatively small sizes at the time.

There are two conclusions that can be drawn from this. First of all, we should note how by making the glass semi-opaque

Van Doesburg tied it as closely as possible to the colour composition of the ensemble and thereby prevented it from appearing as a gap or void. Rather than perceived from the point of view of either structure or function, he ensured the glass staircase was predominantly seen as surface. He made glass and wall interchangeable and, as the 'clothing of space', gave them equal status as mediators between interior and exterior, just as the modern suit was the hinge between outward appearance and inner life. The significance of the staircase as the sole and common circulation route for all occupants of the house should not be forgotten here, nor Van Doesburg's interest in modern clothing as both a tautening and liberating of movement. On the one hand, the whitening of the glass made the staircase more private and brought it further into the body of the house, on the other hand, it drew attention to the role the glass played not only in letting in light but in projecting it. Gispen developed his whitened glass specifically to make his lamps more effective and to cast a more even, diffused light.

The second conclusion is that Van Doesburg's transformation of the glass blurred the roles of the model as a maquette and as a form of architectural representation in its own right, independent of its realization in another form. He thus opened up different possibilities for understanding what the model actually was. In his review of 'Die Wohnung' (1927), Van Doesburg called for a different type of exhibition, one that did not place visitors in front of a series of separated objects. According to Van Doesburg, the spectator should not 'look at' the exhibition but 'experience' it, feel part of it. Indeed, in place of the word 'exhibition', he proposed 'space for demonstration'.[29] By occluding the view into the model by whitening the glass, Van Doesburg deliberately prevented visitors approaching it like a doll's house to be peered into and approached as a miniature version of something else. Instead he presented them with a continuous surface that resisted objectification and concealed its structure. Van Doesburg therefore conceived the model of the Maison d'Artiste as both a model in the sense of a preliminary work, a plan from which a final product could be made, and a model in the sense of an example, an idea about architecture itself. An architecture become entirely surface, which is what the Maison d'Artiste suggests, looked both back to its origins in decoration, as described by Semper, and forwards to a new form of subjectivity that modern life was fashioning.

**22** Gottfried Semper, *Der Stil in den technischen und tektonischen Künsten*, vol. 1 (Frankfurt am Main: Verlag für Kunst und Wissenschaft, 1860), translation: Mallgrave, Robinson 2004. See in particular pp. 242-247. The most significant account of the connection between Semper's theory and the discussion of fashion among modern architects has been given by Wigley 1995.

**23** Theo van Doesburg, letter to J.J.P. Oud, 21 June 1921, quoted by Ex 1996, p. 75.

**24** Mondrian 1919, p. 135.

**25** Theo van Doesburg, 'Stuttgart-Weißenhof 1927: Die Wohnung'. Based on the Dutch translation in: Boekraad (ed.) 1986, p. 167.

**26** Theo van Doesburg, letter to Antony Kok, 18 October 1923. Quoted in Ottevanger 2008, p. 440.

**27** It is strange how little discussion there has been of this model by Van Leusden, who was a 'graficus' and painter, and of the oeuvre of Van Leusden and his contribution to De Stijl. The design for a public transport shelter and design for a urinal, 1922, were depicted in colour in *L'Architecture vivante*, 5 (autumn 1925), fig. 19. See: Kuper 2010, p. 202.

**28** Van Straaten 1988, p. 142.

**29** Theo van Doesburg, 'Stuttgart-Weißenhof 1927: Die Wohnung', Based on the Dutch translation in: Boekraad 1986, p. 164.

10 Reconstruction of the counter-construction of the Maison Particulière at the exhibition 'Theo van Doesburg', Stedelijk Van Abbemuseum, Eindhoven, 1968.

Dolf Broekhuizen

# True-to-life experiences Initiatives for model homes and reconstructions

## The 1:1 experience

Although the drawings and models in the De Stijl exhibition at the Rosenberg gallery in 1923 gave an impression of a possible future architecture, they did not give visitors the full experience of a realized building. They were visualizations of an idea that, over the course of time, themselves attained iconic status. The 'image' played a major role in that. After the Rosenberg exhibition, the isometric projections and the photographs of the models, retouched by Van Doesburg, featured regularly in print. With this expression of an artistic idea, Van Doesburg and Van Eesteren wanted to show what an innovative future architecture might look like. The designers regarded the actual experience of the architecture as important; movement through space and experience of colour were an essential part of the architecture. This kind of experience could be achieved with full-scale exhibitions. Such events were not unknown in the twentieth century. This chapter sketches the context of model homes and housing expos that Van Doesburg and Van Eesteren would have come into contact with at the time. Did Van Doesburg and Van Eesteren perhaps have a wealthy patron in mind as client for the Maison d'Artiste? And what motives played a role later on in full-scale spatial reconstructions?

## Dynamic conception of space

Van Doesburg saw the Maison d'Artiste as his future home. He regarded the design as a proposal for a home-cum-studio where he and his wife, Nelly van Moorsel (1899–1975), could live.[1] The design included a music room for Nelly and for himself a studio with superb natural light from a huge, six-metre-tall window in the north elevation and a lower window in the west elevation providing afternoon light. The building itself brought together music, art and life. At work in the studio Van Doesburg would have been able to hear his wife playing the piano via the staircase, with which most of the rooms were directly connected. Nevertheless, he was aware that it was a dream house, because at that moment, as an artist, he did not have access to the kind of money necessary for such a large structure. He may well have imagined himself as the occupant, but not as a realistic option. The pioneering design for an 'ideal home' that he wrote about in his letters was first and foremost a manifestation of the development of his ideas and those of Van Eesteren.[2]

In essence, the design for the studio dwelling was a demonstration model on several levels: the design was a manifestation of the brief collaboration between artist and architect; it showed what De Stijl was capable of at that moment; and it was part of an architectural exploration by the two designers of a dynamic conception of space. At the time, this conception of space was described as the 'fourth dimension' whereby, moving through the building, a visitor would experience a variety of impressions which afterwards merged into a single overall impression. The sequence of impressions of boundaries, floating volumes, intense, strong colours and the more or less spiral spatial organization alter consciousness, of which a movement through the building and the dimension of time are an essential part.[3]

The fact that the position taken by Van Doesburg and Van Eesteren did not represent a coherent, collective view of architecture on the part of De Stijl, became evident in 1923–1924 in Mondrian's reaction to the Paris exhibition. Whereas for Van Doesburg and Van Eesteren the fourth dimension was linked to an actual experience made up of a succession of impressions in the architecture, for Mondrian the experience of the fourth dimension was more like a kind of clairvoyance.[4]

1 See for example Van Straaten 1988, p. 142.
2 Letter from T. van Doesburg to A. Kok, 18 October 1923, RKD VDA.
3 Blotkamp 1987, p. 76.
4 Blotkamp 1987, p. 76.

Mondrian would not have appreciated the superficial opinion expressed by some reviewers that the models were translations of his paintings into architecture. In an interview, Mondrian criticized the spatial concepts that Van Doesburg was attaching to the models in theoretical texts, for which he had little regard.[5] In response to a question from W.F.A. Roëll, art correspondent for *Het Vaderland* in Paris, who asked whether he approved of 'Van Doesburg and Van Eesteren's floating stacks of coloured blocks', Mondrian was particularly critical of the fourth dimension.[6] He found the models interesting, but primarily as a demonstration; in practice, a lot of improvements would be needed, he wrote a few days after the opening of the exhibition in a letter to J.J.P. Oud.[7] Although Mondrian never allowed himself to be enticed into a collaboration with an architect, his work was not confined to autonomous easel paintings. The walls and interior of his studio in Paris (especially 26 rue du Départ) had been part of his plasticist studies since 1919: a means of expressing 'pure proportion' [fig. 11].[8]

11 Piet Mondrian in his Paris studio, probably photographed by Theo van Doesburg, 1923. On the wall, behind the painting on the easel, coloured planes painted by Mondrian. RKD – Netherlands Institute for Art History, The Hague

## Patron

It is perfectly conceivable that Van Doesburg and Van Eesteren may have regarded the Maison d'Artiste as a real building for their own use, while at the same time designing it as a model home. A client might just turn up in the shape of a (wealthy) patron. This hypothesis is consistent with the work on the Maison Rosenberg, whereby the gallery owner, acting as client, had given De Stijl a platform.[9] In the initial correspondence in 1920, before there was any talk of a building programme, Van Doesburg wrote of a 'model home in the country' and that image stayed with him.[10] Even as work started on the design for the Maison Particulière and the Maison d'Artiste in the summer of 1923, Van Doesburg was writing about 'another model home, that is also intended for exhibition at Rosenberg's gallery'.[11] Van Doesburg revealed in several letters that he preferred to realize his concepts in actual buildings and he tried to win over architects and clients to this idea. It was the strongest argument in his efforts to convince the public of De Stijl's innovations. With a building they could take the public by storm. Evidence of that power of expression within De Stijl were the collaborative projects so far carried out with the likes of J.J.P. Oud.[12]

Van Doesburg and Van Eesteren also noted the way Mondrian used his studio as a promotional tool. The studio was initially known only to artist friends, but in the course of the 1920s, illustrated articles appeared regularly in the press.[13] The austere interior, which Mondrian decorated with a succession of coloured planes intended as an abstract vision of the future, was described as a different world, which left visitors deeply moved by the 1:1 experience. The effect of the photos of the studio was quite different from that of Oud's housing projects, which were in large part tied to practical, functional and structural requirements. Outside De Stijl, the idea for a model home matched the contemporary trend for building and furnishing homes for informational purposes, for example by a local council, housing association or construction company. A full-scale realization would allow visitors to make the acquaintance of De Stijl architecture in a true-to-life manner (spiritually and physically), in a way that was not possible with the models and counter-constructions in the exhibition at the Galerie L'Effort Moderne.

## Housing Expos

In the early twentieth century it was not unusual to hold housing expos that entailed the construction of a full-scale house. Such exhibitions were vehicles for the expression of political ambitions, the promotion of artistic ideas or the demonstration of new techniques. In Germany, for example, where the political climate was oriented towards improving working-class housing, local councils, construction companies and academies built prototypes.[14] model districts in Central Europe. Dutch designers were among the contributors: J.J.P. Oud designed his practical solutions for the minimum dwelling, complete with efficient kitchen, for the City of Stuttgart's Weissenhofsiedlung (1927), and Gerrit Rietveld (1888–1964) built his design for a row of houses for the Wiener Werkbundsiedlung in Vienna (1932) [fig. 13].[20]

Model interiors were also part of the international phenomenon of housing expos. Some were in the nature of an edification

12 Georg Muche and Walter Gropius, Haus am Horn, Weimar, 1923. Model home at the Bauhaus exhibition.

13 The Wiener Werkbundsiedlung on the day of the opening, 4 June 1932. Speeches in front of the row of model houses designed by G.T. Rietveld. Österreichische Nationalbibliothek, Vienna / photo Albert Hilscher

In mid 1923, while Van Doesburg and Van Eesteren were hard at work in Van Doesburg's Paris studio (51 rue du Moulin Vert) preparing for the De Stijl exhibition,[15] a model home was featured in a Bauhaus exhibition held from 15 August to 30 September – two months before the opening of the Rosenberg exhibition – in Weimar.[16] In this Haus am Horn the designers, Georg Muche (1895–1987) and Walter Gropius (1883–1969), combined the classic typology of an atrium house with an industrialized production method made possible by the standardization of building elements [fig. 12].[17] However, owing to its spartan, unornamented exterior, this prototype found little favour with the press.[18] Van Eesteren was already familiar with the project, but Van Doesburg probably did not visit the house until after the De Stijl exhibition: he sketched a picture of it in a letter to Van Eesteren written in November 1923.[19] At the end of the 1920s, early 1930s, various Werkbund (craft) organizations were committed to realizing

**5** For Mondrian's position regarding the fourth dimension, see: Gasten 1978, p. 64.

**6** Anonymous, 17 October 1924; see also Hanssen 2015, p. 212.

**7** Letter from P. Mondrian to J.J.P. Oud, 12 November 1923. See Blotkamp 1978, p. 79.

**8** Blotkamp 1987, pp. 89–101.

**9** In the Netherlands Helene Kröller-Müller was a major patron. In 1911 she commissioned Ludwig Mies van der Rohe (whose photo montage with a design for a skyscraper was on display at Rosenberg's in 1923) and Peter Behrens to make designs for the Ellenwoude country house in Wassenaar. Van der Wolk 1992, pp. 41–46.

**10** Letter from T. van Doesburg to J.J.P. Oud, 19 October 1920, Paris, FC 1972-A.532. See Alied Ottevanger's contribution to this book.

**11** Letter from T. van Doesburg to A. Kok, July 1923, RKD VDA; quoted in Van Straaten 1988, p. 115.

**12** In 1929 Van Doesburg looked back on the early collaborative projects, see White 2011, pp. 48–50.

**13** De Jong 2015, pp. 96–111; for the photographing of Mondrian's studio for promotion purposes see: Manacorda White 2014, pp. 128–141.

**14** Van Andel 2013.

**15** From May 1923 Van Doesburg and his wife Nelly lived in this studio, which he had rented until 15 October 1923. After that he stayed for a month with Mondrian at 26 rue du Départ. Van Eesteren probably arrived in June or July. Van Straaten 1996, pp. 26, 37.

**16** During the 1923 Bauhaus exhibition there were models on show in the exhibition rooms made under the supervision of the lecturers A. Meyer and W. Gropius for a system building method in reaction to Van Doesburg's basic elements. Ex 2000, pp. 77, 100.

**17** The construction of Haus am Horn was less technically experimental than the original plans. Junghanns 1994, pp. 116–118; for steel frame experiments see Junghanns 1994, p. 250 ff.

**18** Jaeggi 2009, pp. 149–153.

**19** Bock reproduces the letter: Bock 2001, p. 206.

**20** Van Andel and Van Gameren 2013, pp. 102–107.

offensive and the events were aimed at imparting good taste to the workers. In 1920, for example, J.J.P. Oud fitted out a model home in Rotterdam's Vreewijk district with relatively inexpensive cane furniture.[21] In the same year Oud, Van Doesburg and Rietveld collaborated on a model interior for Rotterdam's Municipal Housing Agency. For this housing project designed by Oud, Rietveld provided a model interior that included two items that would go on to become world famous, the buffet and

14 Gerrit Rietveld (furniture), Theo van Doesburg (interior colour), J.J.P. Oud (architecture), model interior Spangen housing complex, Rotterdam, 1920
Centraal Museum, Utrecht / photo Ernst Moritz

the so-called red-blue chair, which was at that point probably still unpainted [fig. 14]. The colour design for the interior was by Van Doesburg. For Rietveld the exhibition of the furnishings was one of the most extensive early presentations of his work. The message conveyed by the interior was that even with a limited budget it was still possible to achieve a tasteful (light and spatially open) interior: the straight planks and slats of the furniture were suitable for large-scale machine production and consequently relatively inexpensive.[22] These housing expos had considerable influence on the modernization of the home environment, especially with respect to acceptance by specific target groups. For it was not unknown for a new type of dwelling to be built without first winning over the prospective occupants. One such example was the Bergpolder apartment building in Rotterdam (W. van Tijen, 1933–1934), whose multi-storey set-up had been deemed suitable for singles and 'young couples' (small families).[23]

During this period museums and cultural institutions mounted exhibitions, sometimes in temporary exhibition halls, featuring mock-ups of model homes,[24] which gave an impression of a new type of dwelling, interior or construction method.[25] A well-known example from the modern movement is 'Die Wohnung unserer Zeit' (The Dwelling of Our Time), in which

15 Piet Mondrian's studio, 26 rue du Départ, Paris.
Full-scale reconstruction by Frans Postma, 1994
Research and production: Frans Postma, Delft;
Collection: STAM / photo Fas Keuzenkamp

several leading German designers (Marcel Breuer, Ludwig Hilberseimer, Lilly Reich), supervised by Mies van der Rohe, were able to present their ideas for a new domestic culture with full-scale models displayed in a huge hall in Berlin. This was in 1931, in the midst of the Great Depression. This temporary exhibition, an initiative of the Fachausschuss für Ausstellungsfragen der Bauwirtschaft, was held on a permanent trade fair site in Berlin.[26]

## True-to-life experiences

When De Stijl came to public attention again after the Second World War, consideration was also given to how to make it possible to experience the works of the avant-garde movement in full-scale situations, by means of restorations, open-house events, late realizations and reconstructions. It began with

Mondrian's studio in New York, which was open to the public for six weeks after his death in 1944.[27] In the early 1980s, the Rietveld-Schröder House in Utrecht and Van Doesburg's house in Meudon near Paris were opened to the public.[28] In Strasbourg in 2004, the Dutch state funded the restoration of the Aubette, so that this, too, can be experienced once more.[29] The same objective was behind the restoration (and relocation) in 2015 of a painter's hut in Laren used by Mondrian.[30] Making this piece of heritage accessible in situ is useful, not least because it can be experienced in the original context.

In recent decades museums have launched a number of initiatives aimed at providing a three-dimensional and true-to-life impression of the legacy of De Stijl by means of later reconstructions or installations. There are two reconstructions of Mondrian's studio in Paris, one in Amersfoort (as part of the permanent display in the Mondriaanhuis), and one on tour [fig. 15].[31] Meanwhile, Mondrian's interior design for a library-cum-study for Ida Bienert has been reconstructed no fewer than three times.[32] In undertaking these reconstructions, museums attempt to add a layer to the impression given by the originals. Obviously, such reconstructions are not valued as works of art, but are of an educative or investigative nature.

One of the first exhibitions about De Stijl where specially made mock-ups permitted evocative spatial experiences, was that devoted to the work of Van Doesburg in the Van Abbemuseum in Eindhoven in 1968. Under the guidance of the young

16 General view of the 'Theo van Doesburg' exhibition, Stedelijk Van Abbemuseum, Eindhoven, 1968.
In the background, the reconstruction of the counter-construction of the Maison Particulière.
Van Abbemuseum, Eindhoven / photo Van den Bichelaer, Geldrop

17 Reconstruction of one of the rooms in the Aubette, at the 'Theo van Doesburg' exhibition, Stedelijk Van Abbemuseum, Eindhoven, 1968.
Van Abbemuseum, Eindhoven


**21** Anonymous 1920.
**22** Kuper 1982, pp. 272–274 (1990, pp. 267–269).
**23** In the Bergpolder apartment building two model homes were fitted out, one by Metz & Co and one by Gispen. For model interiors see: Idsinga Schilt 1987, pp. 56–59, 287.
**24** In 1949–1954, the Museum of Modern Art in New York organized exhibitions with model homes in the museum garden and resumed this practice in 2008. Arpa and Van Andel 2013.
**25** A very early, nineteenth-century, model home was built in 1851 on a site next to the World's Fair in the famous Crystal Palace: the 'Prince Albert Model Lodging House'. Van Andel 2013, p. 5.
**26** Van Gameren et al. 2013, p. 92 ff.
**27** De Jong 2015, pp. 179–181.
**28** Van Zijl and Mulder 2009, p. 7; Henket 2004, p. 33.
**29** Guigon et al. 2006.
**30** De Jong 2015; Le Coultre 2015, pp. 84–92.
**31** Postma 1995.
**32** Hanssen 2015, pp. 243–247.

director, Jean Leering, and with the collaboration of Van Eesteren, no fewer than five reconstructions were produced.[33] In order to emphasize the special quality of the new view of architecture, one of the rooms contained, alongside original drawings and photographs, a large model of part of the counter-construction of the Maison Particulière. Visitors were able to wander between and beside the panels, so that they could experience first-hand the spatial quality of the boundaries and colours [figs. 10, 16]. A full-scale reconstruction was made of the flower room in the villa of the Vicomte de Noailles in the southern French town of Hyères (architect Robert Mallet-Stevens), a very small space in which the visitor was surrounded by coloured walls designed in 1925 by Van Doesburg . In addition, two unusual models were made of two of the rooms in the Aubette café-restaurant. The upper part of the walls, including the ceiling, was reconstructed, the lower half of the wall was omitted so that people could walk underneath and, looking up, get an impression of the interior that the clientele of the Strasbourg establishment had briefly been able to experience first-hand [fig. 17]. The actual interior had only a short lifespan because the clients, the brothers Paul and André Horn, quickly replaced Van Doesburg's meticulously designed decor with a new interior.

A fairly large scale had been chosen for the reconstruction of these models in order to facilitate a physical experience. In addition, a scale model of the fountain design for Leeuwarden, approximately 35 cm high, was reconstructed especially for the exhibition, as well as a colour reconstruction of the Maison d'Artiste.[34] The choice of objects was largely determined by the availability of sources for the reconstruction. Several counter-constructions of the Maison Particulière have been preserved in museum collections and archives. Van Eesteren himself collaborated on the reconstruction of the colours of the model of the Maison d'Artiste in order to be able to make a new axonometric projection [fig. 18]. That is noteworthy given that in 1951 he had been so opposed to reconstruction.[35] But in November 1968 Van Eesteren abandoned his reconstruction attempt when it proved impossible to determine the colours.[36]

As well as three-dimensional reconstructions, photographic enlargements are capable of providing quite lifelike impressions. At the Van Doesburg retrospective in Utrecht and Otterlo in 2000, blow-ups of photographs were used to give the impression that Van Doesburg and his work were present. In one more than life-size photograph, he stared at the visitor, his wife and little dog at his side. Excerpts from his pronouncements on the wall gave him a voice as well. The combination of a wall-filling photograph of the interior of the De Stijl exhibition at Léonce Rosenberg's gallery with objects in a display case and furniture, made it seem as if visitors were stepping back in time to 1923, and were present at the Paris exhibition [fig. 19].[37]

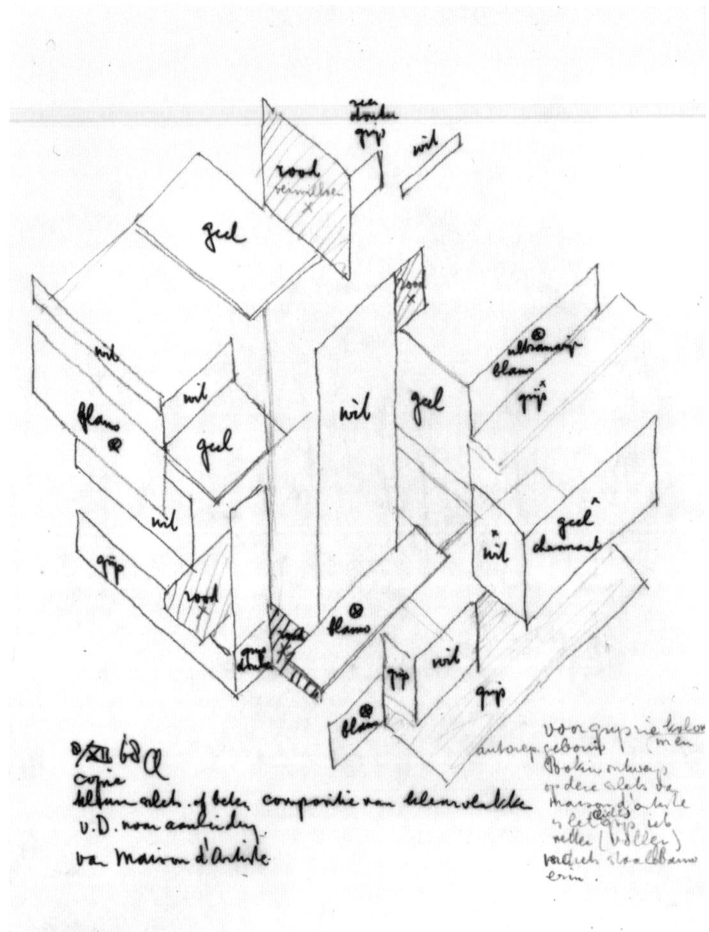

18 C. van Eesteren, Reconstruction of the colour planes of Maison d'Artiste, 1968. The caption includes the following: 'colour sketch, or rather, composition of the colour planes v.D. [van Doesburg] in relation to Maison d'Artiste'. This drawing was used for an axonometric colour reconstruction. Het Nieuwe Instituut, Rotterdam

19 General view of the 'Theo van Doesburg' exhibition, Kröller-Müller Museum Otterlo, 2000, designed by Kossmann.dejong. On the wall an enlargement of the photo of the De Stijl exhibition in 1923. Some of the objects in that photo were on show again, producing a deliberately alienating spatial effect.
Photo Cary Markerink

**33** Leering 1968, pp. 68–69: cat. nos. b27, b36, b39, b52, b57.

**34** With the exception of the Maison d'Artiste and Maison Particulière, these models are in the collection of the Van Abbemuseum, Eindhoven, acquired 1968, inv. nos. 95 (large party room, L'Aubette), 96 (ciné-dancing, L'Aubette), 97 (flower room), 786 (Leeuwarden).

**35** For Van Eesteren's attitude to reconstruction in 1951 see Broekhuizen's contribution in Chapter 7.

**36** For Van Eesteren's reconstruction drawings in 1968: HNI EEST 3.213-3.222.

**37** Kossmann and De Jong 2010, pp. 134–143, 376.

## Marketing or research

What all these initiatives have in common is that they link the educative character to a spatial experience of a full-scale model interior. When the scale of a reconstruction is altered, and the experience of the person present in the space is not paramount, the reconstruction acquires a different character as demonstration model. Thus the model may be a reconstruction component of a design analysis or a teaching project. A case in point is the study that Mick Eekhout, a professor at Delft Technical University, carried out with a group of students. They tried to reconstruct the measurements and colours of the original design of the Maison d'Artiste with the aid of various design drawings and photographs of models. Drawing on the spatial study, they constructed a white 1:5 scale model that was subsequently installed on the Delft campus, thereby making an educational project visible in the public space [fig. 20].[38]

When cultural institutions use the educative character of reconstructions as a marketing concept, they blur the line between reconstruction and a completely new object. In 2009 the Vierkant in Vierkant foundation installed a scale model of Van Doesburg's design for a fountain in Leeuwarden on Leiden's station square in order to draw attention to a Van Doesburg retrospective being held in that city's Stedelijk Museum De Lakenhal. Like the Maison d'Artiste, this 1918 competition design was never realized and was only known from a photo of a model. The temporary object was made in wood, because the permits and financing for a permanent installation in Leiden had proved to be unattainable. The twelve-metre height suggested a scale of 1:1, although the argumentation supporting this is not very robust. In Leeuwarden, the city council reacted to the Leiden initiative by considering a posthumous execution of the design on the site for which it had originally been intended, as part of the programme for Leeuwarden Cultural Capital. But in the end the responsible alderman in Leeuwarden was reluctant to cut across the Leiden initiative and quite quickly abandoned any further planning. Nor are there (as yet) any plans for a permanent realization in Leiden.[39]

In 2015 the Van Eesterenmuseum in Amsterdam presented plans for a scale model of the Maison d'Artiste as part of a sculpture route in the suburban developments designed by Van

20 Model of Maison d'Artiste, construction supervised by Mick Eekhout, research team TU Delft, 1:5, Delft (photo 2016).
This scale model is part of a Delft University of Technology research and educational project.
Photo Dolf Broekhuizen

Eesteren. The plan is to position the four-metre-high model as an eye-catcher beside a yet-to-be built transparent museum pavilion [fig. 21]. Museum director Anouk de Wit sees it as part of a narrative: 'It will become the starting point of the story told by the Westelijke Tuinsteden, with which we want to attract a national and international public.' As an attraction, the scale model can increase the museum's visibility, while on a more substantive level the museum can highlight Van Eesteren's activities as a De Stijl

21 Artist's impression of Van Eesteren Pavilion on Noordzijde, Sloterplas, Amsterdam, Korteknie Stuhlmacher Architecten, 2015. Right, the design for the scale model of the Maison d'Artiste by Victor Veldhuijzen van Zanten. Photomontage Korteknie Stuhlmacher Architecten

architect. The planned realization in 2017 coincides with the celebration of the centenary of De Stijl's formation.[40]

To a certain extent, these scaled-down models, publicity exercises and attractions are not all that far removed from Van Eesteren and Van Doesburg's original idea for a demonstration model and research method. They too reduced it to a scale model and regarded their model as a demonstration of an idea. Of course, the context and the clients are completely different one hundred years later. With the reconstructions, the cultural heritage becomes part of 'the story' of De Stijl in a new way. As always, the quality and rigour of the execution are crucial to the experience of that story.

**38** Eekhout 2000, p. 9; Eekhout 2015, p. 17.

**39** www.vierkantinvierkant.punt.nl (consulted 9 February 2016).

**40** Interview by author with Anouk de Wit, director Van Eesterenmuseum, 8 February 2016.

22 Sketch of Maison Rosenberg in a letter from Theo van Doesburg to A. Kok, 24 February 1921. In letters, Van Doesburg exchanged ideas about the design.
RKD – Netherlands Institute for Art History, The Hague

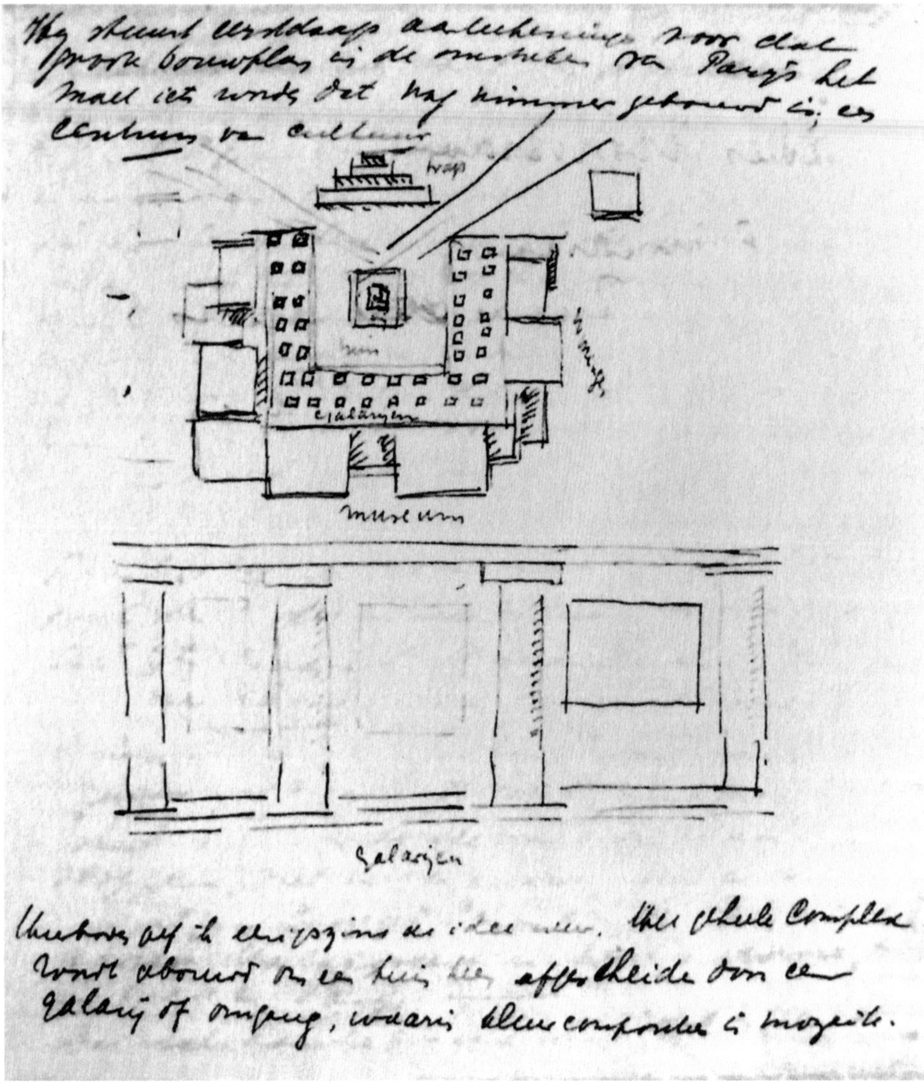

Alied Ottevanger

# Monumental art in models

This chapter focuses more closely on the lead-up to the 'Les Architectes du Groupe "de Styl"' exhibition that took place in the autumn of 1923 at the Galerie L'Effort Moderne in Paris. A detailed examination of this preliminary period, which began in 1919, reveals that the exhibition was primarily the outcome of Theo van Doesburg's unremitting promotion of De Stijl as a group of collaborating artists, and also of his proposal to employ a presentational form that provided a clear prospect of practical implementation.

## Rosenberg for De Stijl

The sequence of events leading up to the exhibition can be clearly followed in the correspondence of Van Doesburg with the French owner of the L'Effort Moderne gallery, Léonce Rosenberg (1879–1947), and with his friend, the architect J.J.P. Oud (1890–1963).[1] [fig. 23] The correspondence with Oud commenced on 30 May 1916, at the beginning of their friendship, and ended with their falling-out in November 1921. The first time that the name Rosenberg is mentioned in Van Doesburg's correspondence with Oud, in March 1919, he is presented as a contributor to the Italian magazine *Valori Plastici*.[2] That he was first and foremost a gallery owner only became clear to Van Doesburg a year later, while he was staying with Mondrian in Paris. He met Rosenberg in person when the latter visited Mondrian's studio. Van Doesburg immediately recognized Rosenberg's potential as a promoter, not just for Mondrian's work, but also for De Stijl. Excited by his success in winning Rosenberg's support for his cause, he wrote to Oud and his wife Annie: 'Dear Friends! ... Rosenberg had to acknowledge that De Stijl's endeavour is the only one for the future and he agreed to an exhibition for next year. There's a great deal for us to do here and I'm planning to live here.'[3]

Back home again in Leiden, Van Doesburg realized that the exhibition Rosenberg had in mind probably related mainly to Mondrian's work, whereas he himself was set on extending it to De Stijl as a whole. He decided to persuade Rosenberg of the importance and significance of this. It should be a manifestation of the essence of De Stijl: the collaboration between painters, sculptors and architects.

Eighteen months earlier, in order to establish the practical feasibility of the De Stijl utopia, Van Doesburg had featured the

23 J.J.P. Oud, posing as architect-artist in Leiden, c. 1917

1 Letters from Léonce Rosenberg to Theo van Doesburg are held in the Van Doesburg Archive (VDA), RKD – Netherlands Institute for Art History, The Hague. The only surviving letter from Van Doesburg to Rosenberg, dated 22 October 1923, is held in the Rosenberg archive, Bibliothèque Kandinsky, Centre Pompidou, Paris. That we know something of Van Doesburg's reactions and proposals is due to the various draft replies and remarks he jotted on Rosenberg's letters. Part of the correspondence between Theo van Doesburg and J.J.P. Oud is held in the Fondation Custodia (FC) in Paris and the VDA, RKD – Netherlands Institute for Art History in The Hague.

2 Letter from T. van Doesburg to J.J.P. Oud, 13 March 1919, VDA, inv. no. 147.

3 Letter from T. van Doesburg to J.J.P. Oud, 7 March 1920, VDA, inv. no. 150.

De Vonk holiday hostel in *De Stijl*. This was the collaborative project that he and Oud had realized in Noordwijkerhout in 1918 [fig. 24]. In his accompanying text, 'Notes on monumental art', he had outlined the ideals that underpinned this work in plain language.[4] A supplement contained photographs of the hall and the corridor in the holiday hostel. As such, the feature article demonstrated the theory and practice of cooperation between painter and architect.

Oud on 11 May 1920 that: 'The article "L'Art Monumental" has already had an effect. From Rosenberg, the man who is launching the new in Paris and is very supportive of our cause, I received an enthusiastic missive. I replied at length: that it was not utopian, but that we, on however small a scale, had put it into practice etc. ...'[6]

It is clear from the earliest surviving letter from Rosenberg to Van Doesburg, dated July 1920, that by then at any rate

24 T. van Doesburg and J.J.P. Oud, hall of De Vonk holiday hostel, Noordwijkerhout, 1918. Supplement 1 of *De Stijl* November 1918. This project, featured in *De Stijl,* showed that in concrete projects, collaboration between painter and architect was realistic.

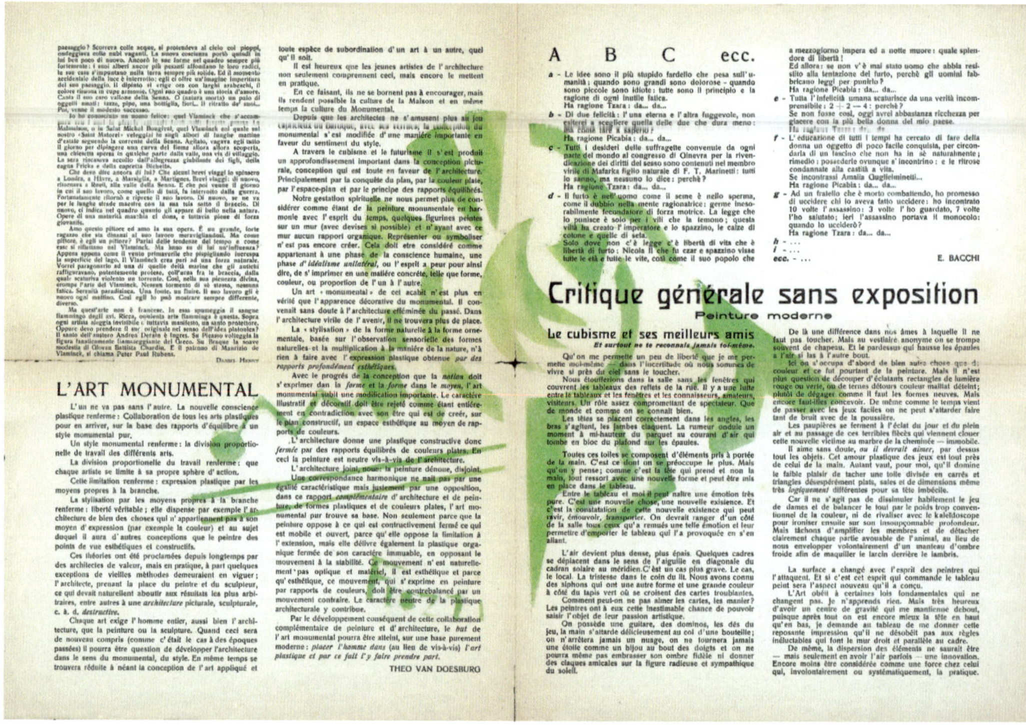


25 Theo van Doesburg, 'L'Art Monumental', *Bleu*, July 1920
RKD – Netherlands Institute for Art History, The Hague

## Promotion with the pen

To publicize De Stijl's pursuit of collaboration between artists and architects outside the Netherlands, Van Doesburg had 'Notes on monumental art' translated into French, presumably shortly after his return from Paris. The resulting article, 'L'Art monumental', was subsequently offered to various foreign magazines, with some success. In April 1920 it was published in *Lumière* and shortly thereafter in *Bleu* and *Terramar.*[5] [fig. 25]

Presumably anticipating the facts, Van Doesburg wrote to

Rosenberg had indeed been won over. He had read 'L'Art monumental' in the June issue of *Terramar* and expressed great interest.[7] Van Doesburg was naturally delighted with this effect of his publishing offensive and immediately apprised Oud of his success: 'My "L'Art monumental" article has appeared in all those foreign magazines, however without reproductions! No doubt because of the expensive plates! Yesterday evening there was a letter from Rosenberg (the great!) in Paris, who is ecstatic about my ideas and has sent the article to his friends. Nice, don't you think?'[8]

## Architect–painter collaboration

The main aim of Van Doesburg's article was to show that collaboration among artists was a pre-condition for achieving a monumental style. In *De Stijl* he had put it this way: 'The new expressive consciousness signifies: collaboration of all plastic arts to attain, on the basis of balanced relationships, a pure monumental style.

'A monumental style signifies: proportionate division of labour of the various arts. Proportionate division of labour signifies that every artist restricts himself to his own field. This restriction signifies: expression using discipline-specific means.'[9]

Thus the architect should not concern himself with colour. That belonged to the domain of the painter, who in turn should leave the design of the building, the determination of volumes, to the architect. It was this balanced collaboration that resulted in the desired objectives: 'Architecture has a structural, thus closed plasticity [while ...] painting [produces] an open plasticity through two-dimensional colour expression.' In that way painting also generated movement in architecture.[10]

In *De Stijl* these matters had been demonstrated by means of pictures of 'architectural fragments': the first-floor corridor and the ground-floor hall of the holiday hostel. Those reproductions were lacking in the French publications. Probably because of this, the French article ended with the more general exhortation directed at architects and painters to work together on a purely modern basis (the absolutely balanced collaboration) to develop a monumental art. In conclusion, individuals or users were called upon to draw inspiration from the plasticism and participate actively in this monumental art. In other words, they should consciously adapt their living and working behaviour to the environment that was designed according to these principles.

## Demonstration in Paris

During Oud's August 1920 trip to Paris, he did not succeed in visiting Rosenberg. There were other setbacks, too, but Van Doesburg steadfastly continued to explore possibilities for a De Stijl exhibition in Paris, even though the gallery owner did not have an opening for it in the short term: 'Rosenberg ... is willing. Wrote that he is very sorry not to have met you because he would so like to meet one of the arch pioneers of the new civilization. He said that there's not much opportunity for implementing the new in Paris either, because Paris is still completely in thrall to the 18th century. ... I'm now busy winning over France. ... Every day, every hour I see it clearly, it's first and foremost a matter establishing a new attitude to life. It's not a question of making a house or a painting a bit differently than previously. The old has to be radically demolished, at the same time as the new is being built up.'[11]

Van Doesburg's persistence eventually paid off. Rosenberg suggested that he design for him – as soon as it was possible – a model country house. Needless to say, Van Doesburg immediately took up his pen to discuss this fantastic plan with Oud: 'Dear chap! I've got wonderful news! Just received a very interesting letter from Léonce Rosenberg.[12] He asks me to send him photographs of all your works. He wants, as soon as the fin situation has improved a bit (he writes of a few years' time) to build a model home in the country with the collaboration of the De Stijl artists. He wants to realize our ideas fully in it! He also wants a completely modern garden etc. ... This could turn out to be a demonstration with which we **knock them all dead**!! Come and talk about it soon.'[13]

## Designs + model

Van Doesburg was also wildly enthusiastic about this prospect in his response to Rosenberg. He wrote that his friend Oud (photographs of whose work he had meanwhile sent to Paris) was equally keen about the idea. As far as he was concerned the preparation of their exhibition should not be long delayed. And then Van Doesburg made a surprising suggestion: 'My friend Oud, who was in Leiden a few days ago, was like me very enthusiastic about your project for an exhibition of our ideas in France. It's a real pity that we cannot start work immediately,

4 [T. van Doesburg] 'Aanteekeningen over monumentale kunst', *De Stijl*, II (1918) no. 1 (November), pp. 10-12 and supplement 1.

5 See *Lumière* April 1920; *Terramar* II (June 1920) 23/24; *Bleu* 1 (July 1920). The last two are in the VDA, see inv. nos. 669 and 662. In 1922, the article appeared once more in Russian, in *Vesc = Objet = Gegenstand*, nos. 1-2 (March-April) see VDA, inv. no. 680.

6 Letter from T. van Doesburg to J.J.P. Oud, 11 May 1921, FC 1972 A.518.

7 Letter from L. Rosenberg to T. van Doesburg, 26 July 1920, VDA, inv. no. 178 and cf. *Terramar* II (June 1920) 23/24, pp. 3-4, VDA, inv. no. 669.

8 Postcard from T. van Doesburg to J.J.P. Oud, 28 July 1920, VDA, inv. no. 150.

9 See note 4, p. 10 in *De Stijl* 2 (1918) 1 (November).

10 Ibid.

11 Letter from T. van Doesburg to J.J.P. Oud, 1 October 1920, FC 1972 A.531(6).

12 Refers to Rosenberg's letter of 16 October 1920, VDA inv. no. 178.

13 Letter from T. van Doesburg to J.J.P. Oud, 19 October 1920, FC 1972-A.532. NB note on envelope in ballpoint: 'the start of the Rosenberg house in Paris!'

but now at least we have time to prepare well, for such an exhibition must be a perfect and durable example of the modern Style. I sincerely hope that realization will not be long delayed, a model for the project could be made in advance in order to give an overall impression.'[14]

Van Doesburg's suggestion to make a model of the project so as to give an impression of the totality beforehand was well received. Rosenberg reciprocated by offering to shoulder the

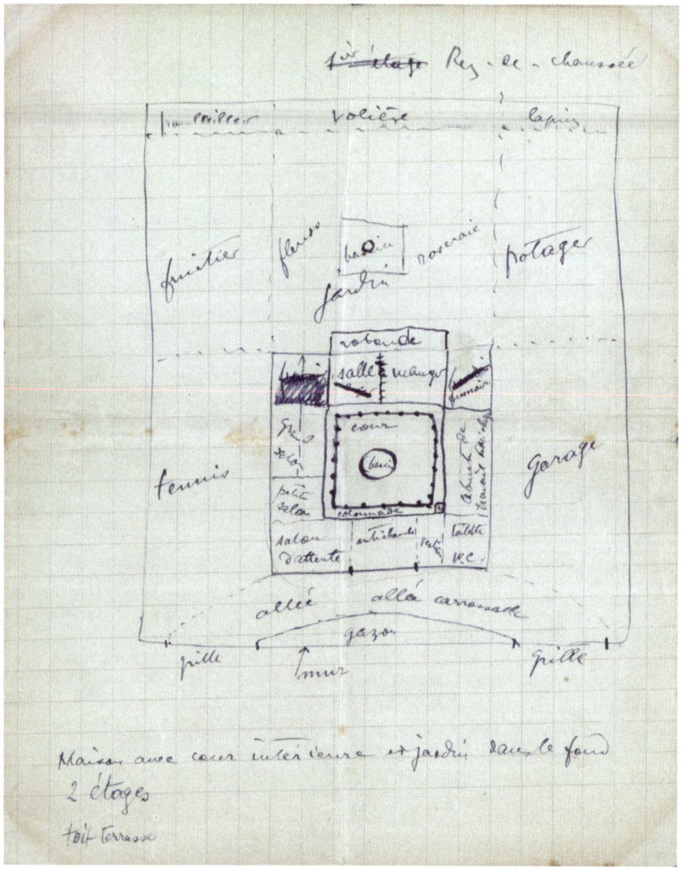


26, 27, 28 L. Rosenberg, design sketch Maison Rosenberg, ground floor, 1921. One of the drawings with a programme for the model house, drawn up by Rosenberg., Left: ground floor, middle: first and second floors, right: third floor and basement. Fondation Custodia, Paris. Collection Frits Lugt

costs of the exhibition: 'If you and Mr Oud wish to make models representing your constructions and your interiors in miniature, I would be disposed to exhibit them here next year at my expense.'[15]

Because Rosenberg wrote that he wanted to hold the exhibition the following year, Van Doesburg suggested to Oud at the beginning of that year, 1921, that they should discuss the idea. This became somewhat urgent when Rosenberg announced that he was coming to Amsterdam, where he wanted to speak to Van Doesburg.[16] After this meeting, which took place on Monday 21 February, Van Doesburg reported to Oud: 'Over dinner in "Polmanshuis" we discussed the question of the house at length.

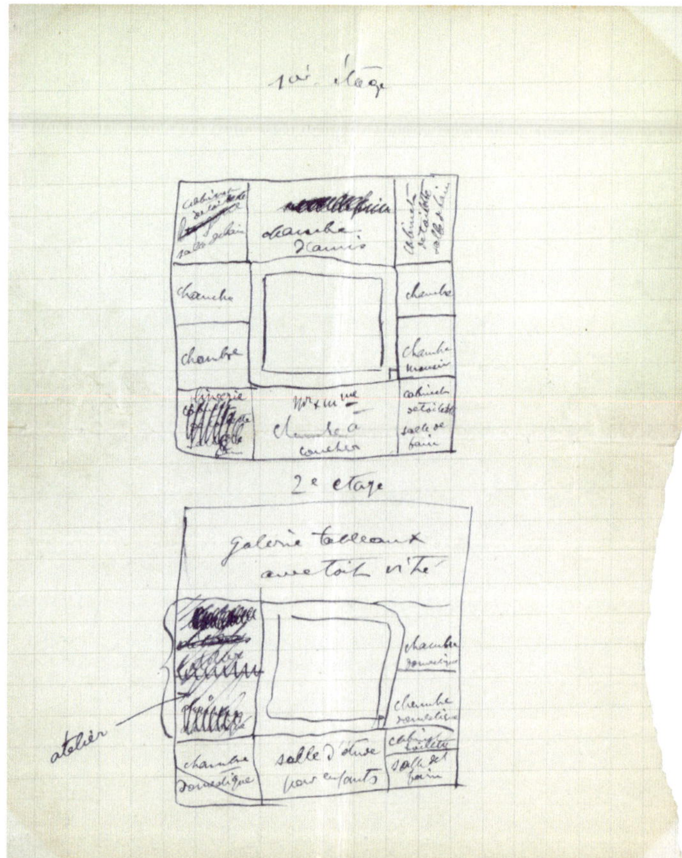


His intention is to commission a residence with a garden in the form of a courtyard, closed off by a gallery. I'm expecting to receive all the details about the layout soon, after which we can make a start on the design and model. It's also his plan to exhibit these designs + model in his depots in London, America etc (at his expense), however we have to defray the cost of the model etc.'[17]

## It should act as a bomb

When Van Doesburg was in Paris again in April, they fleshed out the plan in more detail, with Rosenberg making a few clarifying sketches: [figs. 26, 27, 28] 'Rosenberg has given me a full explanation of his intention and all the points were dealt with. He even made a few "rough sketches" of the layout of the house in question. You'll find them enclosed.[18] ... Study these sketches at your leisure and ... remember that they are not binding.

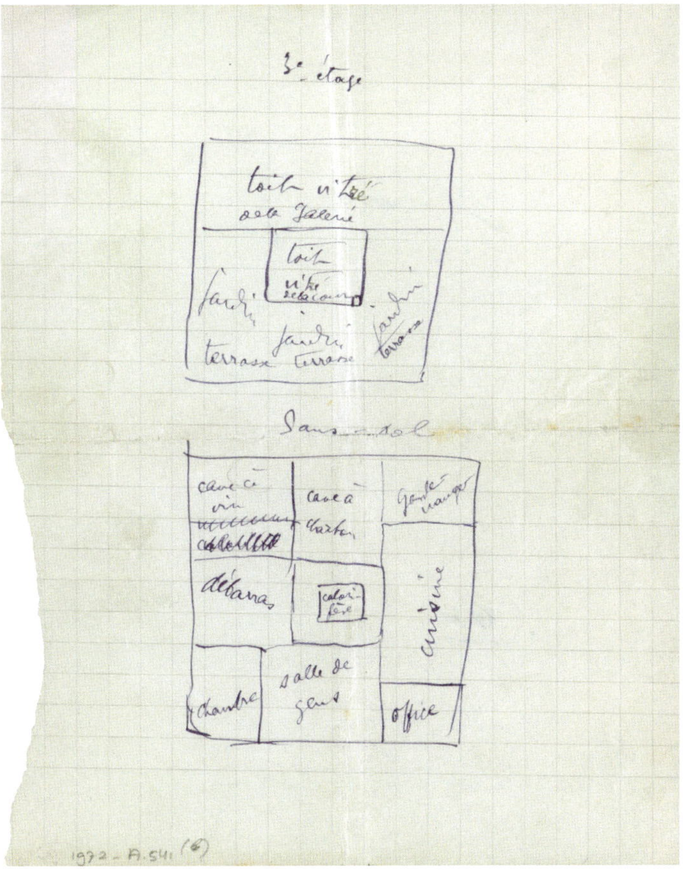


Rosenberg allows us freedom in everything and these sketches are only intended to indicate what kind of rooms etc should be included. He wanted to start with the exhibition in Jan. or Feb. 1922 and is very, exceptionally enthusiastic about the matter. He assures us that our work will have positive results, that it should act as a bomb that blows everything that happens here apart. The exhibition will consist of: a. all the designs and photographs of the architecture and painting relating to this building; b. examples of details in model form and executed stained-glass windows. Furthermore and primarily a single model, made up of various pieces, which can be taken apart in order to see the construction as well as the internal sections.'[19]

Nothing more happened for the rest of that year, or in 1922, even after what seemed like a breakthrough in January when Rosenberg sent his typed layout for the projected house.[20] It was not until November 1922 that the plans were revisited and the contributions of other De Stijl artists addressed explicitly. Van Doesburg and his group were to be responsible for the artworks: the designs, models and photographs plus the cost of their transport and insurance. Rosenberg would provide the exhibition space and pay for the invitations and suchlike. He reiterated these arrangements: 'I am still prepared to exhibit what we discussed in 1921 and as testimony to the sympathy I feel for your projects, I would not charge your group for the

**14** 'Mon ami Oud qui était à Leyde il y a quelques jours était tout aussi bien que moi, très enthousiaste de votre projet d'une manifestation de nos ideés [idées, transl.] en France. C'est bien dommage que nous ne pouvons pas tout de suite commencer le travail, mais maintenant nous avons au moins le temps de nous bien préparer car une telle manifestation faut être un exemple parfait et durable du Style moderne. J'espère bien que la réalisation ne se fera pas attendre trop longtemps, une maquette d'après le projet pourrait être faire [faîte, transl.] d'avance pour donner une impression totale.' Van Doesburg wrote this draft – which he dated 24 October 1920 – in the margin on the back of Rosenberg's letter to him, dated 16 October 1920, see note 12.

**15** 'Si vous et monsieur Oud vouliez exécuter des maquettes représentant vos constructions et vos intérieurs en miniature, je serais disposé à eu [en, transl.] faire ici d'exposition [l'exposition, transl.] à mes frais l'année prochaine.' Letter from L. Rosenberg to T. van Doesburg, 7 February 1921, VDA, inv. no. 178.

**16** Rosenberg had an appointment with Mak van Waay, director of the Amsterdam auction house where, a year earlier, on 13 January 1920, he had auctioned part of his collection of Asian art and on 1 June 1920 medieval art and antiquities. On 22 February and 19 October 1921, a group of modern and cubist artworks owned by Rosenberg went under the hammer at this auction house.

**17** Letter from T. van Doesburg to J.J.P. Oud, which can be dated around the end of February 1921, FC-1972-A580 (2).

**18** Those 'rough sketches' of Rosenberg's are preserved with the letter from T. van Doesburg to J.J.P. Oud, April 1921, which can be placed at the beginning of that month, FC-1972-A541 (2). Rosenberg sketched floor plans on two sheets of squared paper, FC-1972-A541 (a, b). These sketches make a somewhat more classic, more closed impression than the earlier sketches Van Doesburg had made of what he described as 'a centre of culture', in his letter to Kok, 24 February 1921. See fig. 22. See Ottevanger 2008, p. 316.

**19** See the letter referred to in note 17.

**20** This typescript is of the Dutch translation, dated 3 January 1922, VDA, inv. no. 178.

exhibition space nor invitation cards. You would only have to pay the return cost of transporting your plans, models, photographs etc ... .'[21]

### Friendship and rift

Ever since their initial contact, relations between Van Doesburg and Rosenberg had been cordial and they performed favours for one another. Thus Van Doesburg published Rosenberg's 'Parlons Peinture' series of articles in *De Stijl*. For his part, Rosenberg published Van Doesburg's *Classique-Baroque-Moderne* as a L'Effort Moderne edition.

The friendship with Oud, however, sustained serious damage in the autumn of 1921. In the last instance, Oud was unwilling to implement Van Doesburg's colour designs for the social housing estate he was designing for Rotterdam's Spangen district, in accordance with the painter's directions. That was completely unacceptable for Van Doesburg. He stood by his principle that in their collaboration to achieve a monumental art, the architect and painter should each contribute according to their own field of expertise. Following a furious row, this culminated in November 1921 in a rift between the friends that was never healed. From that day forward, their ways parted.

### New recruits and absentees

In spring 1922, Oud contacted Rosenberg directly. When he received confirmation of his suspicion that while Rosenberg did have an ideal house in mind, there was no question of an actual commission, he withdrew from this project. Van Doesburg found himself obliged to consider other architects. Fortunately, in early May the young architect Cornelis van Eesteren arrived on the scene and Van Doesburg recognized his talent straight away. For his part, Van Eesteren felt an immediate affinity with Van Doesburg and readily agreed to his proposal for collaboration [fig. 29].

Apart from Van Doesburg and Cornelis van Eesteren, Rosenberg's letter of 27 January 1923 named Jan Wils and Gerrit Rietveld as participants in the exhibition.[22] They were indeed involved in the exhibition, to which everyone made different contributions. Although Oud's name was missing, he was in fact represented

29 Cornelis van Eesteren (left), Nelly van Doesburg (centre) and Theo van Doesburg (right) in Paris, 1923
Het Nieuwe Instituut, Rotterdam

by seven photographs of realized architectural projects.

Nor was there any mention of Mondrian in Rosenberg's letter and he was the only one who really did remain outside the exhibition. Although Van Doesburg had suggested that he provide a colour design for the models at his own discretion, Mondrian had too little confidence in architecture and declined the proposal.

and the Maison d'Artiste. These models, designed and built in strict accordance with the ideals of Van Doesburg and Van Eesteren, demonstrated that the collaboration between painter and architect was a precondition for achieving De Stijl's sought-after monumental style. And as a means of providing a persuasive impression of the practical feasibility of this ideal, the models proved to be exceptionally effective.

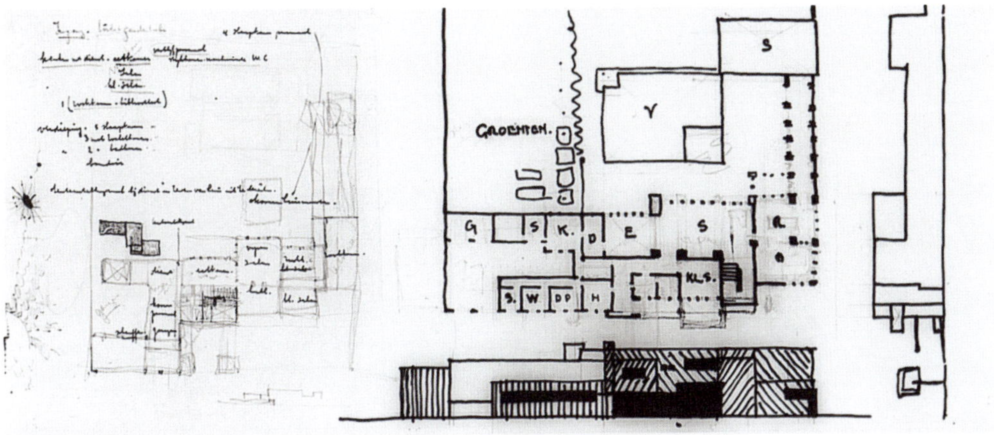

30 C. van Eesteren, design sketch for the Maison Rosenberg, 1923, floor plans, front elevation and one of the side elevations. Het Nieuwe Instituut, Rotterdam

GALERIE "L'EFFORT MODERNE"
LÉONCE ROSENBERG
19, Rue de La Baume — Paris (VIII<sup>e</sup>)

*rez-de-chaussée*

**Les Architectes du Groupe "de Styl"**
*(HOLLANDE)*

PROJETS ET MAQUETTES PAR

THÉO VAN DOESBURG, C. VAN EESTEREN, HUSZAR
W. VAN LEUSDEN, J.-J. P. OUD, G. RIETVELD,
MIES VAN DER ROHE, WILS.

Exposés du 15 Octobre au 15 Novembre 1923
de 10 h. à 12 h. et de 14 h. à 17 h. 30
*(dimanches et fêtes exceptés)*

INVITATION

31 Invitation, Les Architectes du Groupe "de Styl", Galerie L'Effort Moderne, Paris, 1923 Het Nieuwe Instituut, Rotterdam

## Three models, two winners

In May 1923 it turned out that the only possible time slot Rosenberg had for the De Stijl exhibition that year was the period 15 October to 15 November. And that was indeed the precise duration of the exhibition [fig. 31].

At the 'Les Architectes du Groupe "de Styl"' exhibition in Rosenberg's Galerie L'Effort Moderne, the model of the Maison Rosenberg, which was the largest of the three models, occupied centre stage. The floor plans had been drawn by Van Eesteren. Compared with earlier sketches by Rosenberg and Van Doesburg, Van Eesteren's design featured an extension and in particular a more varied articulation of volumes [fig. 30]. Although the intention in January 1923 had still been to have Rietveld determine the furniture and interior and Mondrian and Van Doesburg the colours, the eventual model (made by Rietveld) was white and unfurnished and that was how it was exhibited. However, it was not this large, imposing model that stole the show, but two other, smaller and coloured models: those of the Maison Particulière

**21** 'Je suis toujours disposé à faire l'exposition dont nous avions parlé en 1921 et pour vous témoigner toute la sympathie que je porte à vos projets, je ne compterai à votre groupement aucun frais de location ni de cartes d'invitation. Vous n'auriez donc à supporter que les frais d'aller et retour de vos plans, maquettes, photos etc...' Letter from L. Rosenberg to T. van Doesburg, 9 November 1922, VDA, inv. no. 178.

**22** See VDA, inv. no. 178.

32 Cornelis van Eesteren (left) and Theo van Doesburg (right) posing beside the model of Maison Particulière in the studio in Paris, 1923
Het Nieuwe Instituut, Rotterdam

Kees Somer

# 'We worked ever more fully together' Van Eesteren and the 'collective construction'

## Inspiration from collaboration

The Maison d'Artiste was the high point of the collaboration between Van Doesburg and Van Eesteren in Paris. Their design for the studio house was a conceptual realization of De Stijl's pursuit of a synthesis of painting and architecture in a harmonious, abstract living environment. Drawing on the complementarity of painter and architect, Van Doesburg and Van Eesteren achieved such a synergy and integration of ideas that the result was more than the sum of their individual efforts. The high expectations these designers had of their interactive work practice are consistent with insights into social dynamics and collaboration that developed within the behavioural sciences from the 1930s onwards. Van Eesteren drew a great deal of inspiration from that short-lived collaboration in 1923 and for the rest of his working life he chose to work as part of a team [fig. 32]. Underpinning this was his conviction that a universally valid contemporary vision of the living environment could only emerge from a collective work practice. He used his position as chairman of the international architects' organization CIAM, to propagate and practise the principle of collectivity, working in concert with the secretary Sigfried Giedion. Whether it concerned an artwork, an urban development plan or an association like that of CIAM, what mattered for Van Eesteren was that it should be conceived in a process of 'collective construction' as a prefiguration of a society in which art and life would be integrated.

## Magazines, manifestos, exhibitions

Friendship, trust and mutual support. These, the German art critic Adolf Behne (1885–1948) opined shortly after the First World War, were the absolute preconditions for collaboration between progressive artists and architects. Behne was reacting to a survey that the Berlin Arbeitsrat für Kunst (a union of architects, artists and art critics) had sent to its members in 1919 in order to canvass their opinion about the desirability of international collaboration.[1] History would prove him right, for the years that followed showed just how difficult it was for the avant-garde to organize itself constructively and lastingly. Not that there was any shortage of attempts. In 1918 a number of artists and architects had already pushed for the formation of 'an international unity in Life, Art and Culture' in the first manifesto published in the avant-garde magazine *De Stijl*.[2] A year later, at the other end of the artistic spectrum, the aforementioned (expressionist) Arbeitsrat für Kunst called on artists everywhere to usher in a structural collaboration with an international congress. The 1920s, too, saw many such initiatives, which usually fell victim to internal discord or lack of trust. It was not until 1928 that progressive architects in Europe, at least, succeeded in organizing in the Congrès Internationaux d'Architecture Moderne (CIAM).

Nevertheless, some smaller artistic collaborative ventures were established, sometimes in connection with the publication of a magazine, the organization of an exhibition or the drafting of a manifesto. These alliances often had a floating membership and a short lifespan. In the case of De Stijl, however, the lifespan was quite long, at least if we date its inception from the first issue of the eponymous magazine in 1917 and identify its end with the death of its founder Theo van Doesburg in 1931. But De Stijl was not a homogeneous group that operated jointly. It was primarily a project of the indefatigable Van Doesburg, who succeeded in involving an array of like-minded individuals for varying periods in his artistic, publicity and propaganda activities. In the aforementioned first manifesto (1918), the signatories announced their collective commitment to the fusion of painting and architecture in the total artwork of the coloured abstract living environment. The ultimate goal of their mission was to see

1 Schlösser et al. 1980, p. 20.

2 The signatories of the first De Stijl manifesto were: Theo van Doesburg, Robert van 't Hoff, Vilmos Huszár, Anthony Kok, Piet Mondriaan, Georges Vantongerloo, Jan Wils; Van Doesburg et al. 1918-b, p. 2.

the arts united in constructive harmony as a harbinger of a radical new society.[3] The aesthetic principles for an uncompromising stylistic purity were morally justified by regarding them as instruments of social reform. This called for a systematic, almost scientific, inquiry into the foundations of the design, by individuals trained in its various aspects. Architects, painters, sculptors and poets were required to work together on the creation of a harmonious living environment, in which their contributions, based on common objectives and stylistic features, would coalesce.

33 Cornelis van Eesteren and Theo van Doesburg with artist friends in Weimar, 1922. Het Nieuwe Instituut, Rotterdam

## Vers une construction collective

In the event, the De Stijl artists' opinions on the relation between architecture and the arts proved to be too diverse for the formation of a structural collaboration. There were occasional projects in which they did come close to the desired artistic synthesis. The collaboration between Van Doesburg and Van Eesteren in the summer of 1923 produced new insights. During their collaborative work on Van Eesteren's design for a university hall in Amsterdam they came to the conclusion that a new spatial experience was possible when the architecture allowed itself to be influenced by the art of painting.[4] With the new experience of total space, the relation between architect and painter changed. Colour no longer served to accentuate surfaces, but could invest the design with a connective continuity independent of the architectural structure. The growing understanding of the spatial possibilities of colour and the desire to fully integrate colour and architecture, led in the early 1920s to greater equality between painter and architect. The basis for that successful collaboration between Van Doesburg and the fifteen years younger Van Eesteren, who had met in Weimar in 1922 [fig. 33], was the complementarity of artist and architect: Van Doesburg strove to realize De Stijl in architecture, Van Eesteren was able to correlate his ideas about colour and space with other form-defining factors like function and construction. The result was a joint exploration of the boundaries between visual art and architectural design, in an increasingly intense creative process that in 1923 culminated in the Maison d'Artiste. In 1924, the duo published the foundations of the new architecture in *De Stijl*, in a manifesto and an explanation with the programmatic title: 'Vers une construction collective' [fig. 34]. Through the rhetorical use of the 'we' form, they highlighted the method of collaborative analysis and 'plastic expression' (*beelding*) and made it clear that only in the context of a harmonious collaboration could the form of expression of the new era be developed.[5]

## We worked ever more fully together

Van Doesburg and Van Eesteren's collaboration on the Paris models in the studio at 51 rue du Moulin Vert, has fired the imagination ever since the opening of the exhibition 'Les Architectes du Groupe "de Styl"' in 1923 [figs. 35, 36, 37]. The reason for this is not only the groundbreaking nature of their architectural experiments, but doubtless also curiosity about an interactive creative process that has never been fully explained. In 2001 this collaboration was comprehensively analysed by Manfred Bock, who based his work on earlier studies by, among others, Jean Leering, Yve-Alain Bois, Nancy Troy and Evert van Straaten.[6] Bock distinguished two extreme standpoints in the debate: on the one hand, Van Doesburg as creative spirit and Van Eesteren who concretized his ideas architecturally, and on the other hand, Van Eesteren as designer and Van Doesburg who coloured the planes of the models and drawings. Between these extremes

**VERS UNE CONSTRUCTION COLLECTIVE**

**(MANIFESTE V DU GROUPE "DE STIJL")**

G. RIETVELD

THÉO VAN DOESBURG

VAN EESTEREN

I — En travaillant collectivement, nous avons examiné l'architecture comme unité créée de tous les arts, industrie, technique, etc... et nous avons trouvé que la conséquence donnera un style nouveau.

II — Nous avons examiné **les lois de l'espace** et leurs variations infinies (c'est-à-dire les contrastes d'espaces, les dissonances d'espaces, les compléments d'espaces etc... et nous avons trouvé que toutes ces variations de l'espace sont à gouverner comme une unité équilibrée.

III — Nous avons examiné **les lois de la couleur** dans l'espace et dans la durée et nous avons trouvé que les rapports équilibrés de ces éléments donnent enfin une unité nouvelle et positive.

IV — Nous avons examiné le rapport entre l'espace et le temps, et nous avons trouvé que l'apparition de ces deux éléments par la couleur donne une nouvelle dimension.

V — Nous avons examiné les rapports réciproques de la mesure, de la proposition, de l'espace, du temps et des matériaux et nous avons trouvé la méthode définitive de les construire comme une unité.

VI — Nous avons par la rupture de la fermeté (les murs etc...) élevé la dualité entre l'intérieur et l'extérieur.

VII — Nous avons donné la vraie place de la couleur dans l'architecture et nous déclarons que la peinture séparée de la construction architecturale (c'est-à-dire le tableau) n'a aucune raison d'être.

VIII — L'époque de la destruction est totalement finie. Une nouvelle époque commence, celle de la **construction**.

Paris 1923.

34 'Vers une Construction Collective', Manifesto 5 of De Stijl, Paris 1923. Distributed in 1923 as a pamphlet at the exhibition in Galerie L'Effort Moderne, published the following year in *De Stijl*. Het Nieuwe Instituut, Rotterdam

**3** See also Troy 1979; Somer 2007, pp. 68–79.

**4** Bock 2001, p. 145.

**5** Van Doesburg and Van Eesteren 1924. The model of Maison Rosenberg shown in the pamphlet was made by Rietveld.

**6** Bock 2001, pp. 151–195.

there are numerous viewpoints, the most popular being a gradual diminution in Van Eesteren's contribution: Van Eesteren designed the Maison Rosenberg (Hôtel Particulier), they worked together on the Maison Particulière and Van Doesburg made the Maison d'Artiste.[7] Bock, however, reached a different conclusion, namely that the final project was in fact the high point of their collaboration. He based his conclusion on Van Eesteren's own reading of the course of events, and argued at length for the correctness of this interpretation.

After 1923 Van Eesteren occasionally spoke about his collaboration with Van Doesburg. In 1951 he looked back on it in a letter to the Swiss art historian, Sigfried Giedion (1888–1968). He pointed out that Van Doesburg and he had both signed their Parisian creations. According to him the three houses in the exhibition represented three phases in their creative work: he had made Hôtel Particulier on his own, for the Maison Particulière he

35 Cornelis van Eesteren working on the model of Maison Particulière, Paris, 1923
Het Nieuwe Instituut, Rotterdam

had designed the house and Van Doesburg had done the colours, and the Maison d'Artiste they had created together by way of a process of 'mutual permeation'.[8] Around the same time, in a letter to Willem Sandberg (1897–1984), director of Amsterdam's Stedelijk Museum, he revealed more details about this gradually intensified collaboration. According to Van Eesteren, Van Doesburg had determined the colours of the second and third house and applied them to the models, respectively 'in close contact' and 'in close collaboration' with him; 'it was the same as with the spatial aspect of designing. We worked ever more fully together'.[9] For this final, most intensive form of collaboration, Van Eesteren used the expression 'mutual permeation'. The joint activities were not determined by a division of labour based on competence, but by a common thought and design process capable of leading to unprecedented and unforeseen results. For Van Eesteren, as he wrote to Van Doesburg a year after the Paris adventure, their collaboration had not resulted in 'a sum of capabilities: *C.v.E. + Does* or *Does + C.v.E.*, but a *new entity*, a new manifestation, that we have both brought to life … when *we* work together the result is not a doubling of strength, of energy, but an x-fold of our combined individual strength … In this way, our collaboration became non-personal.'[10]

## Developmental psychology

As far as Van Eesteren was concerned, the value of his cooperation with Van Doesburg lay in the unfathomable mutual cross-fertilization, which generated a productive and unpredictable –

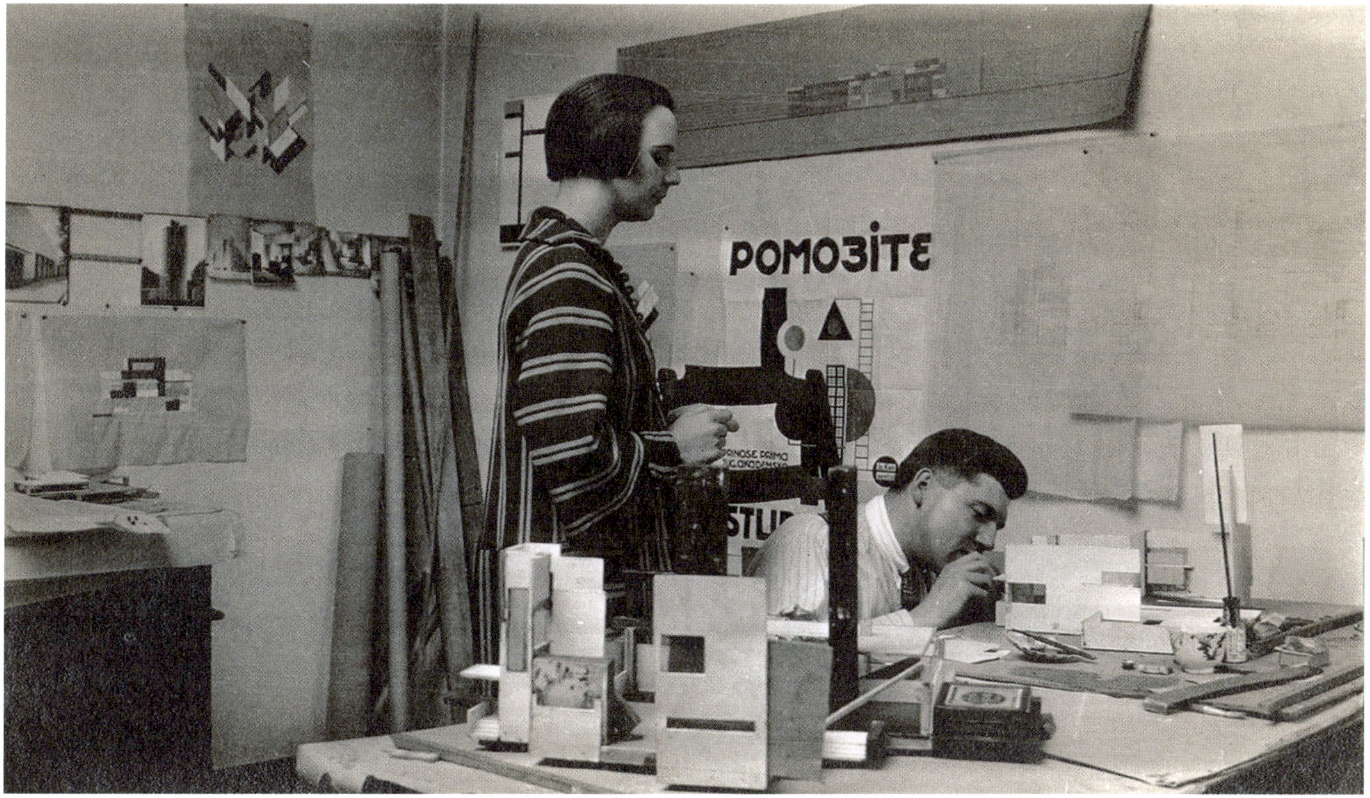


36 Cornelis van Eesteren working on components for the model of Maison Particulière in the studio in Paris, 1923. Left, Nelly van Doesburg
Het Nieuwe Instituut, Rotterdam

7 Bock 2001, p. 155.
8 In German, 'gegenseitige Durchdringung'. Letter from C. van Eesteren to S. Giedion, 29 May 1951. Quoted in Bock 2001, p. 156.
9 Letter from C. van Eesteren to W. Sandberg, 2 July 1951. Quoted in Bock 2001, p. 156.
10 Letter from C. van Eesteren to T. van Doesburg, 15 August 1924. Quoted in Jaffé 1983, p. 85.

and therefore 'non-personal' – synergy that allowed them to break new ground and convincingly take the design to a higher plane. This view is strikingly similar to insights that were evolving around the same time in the emergent discipline of social psychology. Rather than regarding human beings primarily as individuals, it saw them as part of a more or less organized community. In the beginning, the main impetus came from developmental psychology, which conducted empirical research into the social behaviour of children in relation to their surroundings. If the focus was initially on the individual as actor within a group, in the 1930s it switched to collective work per se. One interesting example is a 1937 study of collaboration by the Dutch developmental psychologist Maria Bos (1899–1973), titled *Experimental Study of Productive Collaboration* [fig. 38].[11] She defined group work as work that two or more people carry out together in such a way that all have an equal share in it and exchange ideas without reverting to a simple division of tasks. In other words, she was interested in genuinely collective work. Bos studied the associated mutual contact and its effects, an approach that she claimed to have encountered in only one earlier publication.[12] The most important question she raised, was how group work related to individual work. And more especially: did collaboration lead to better outcomes and, if so, were they the sum or the synthesis of individual activities? In order to be able to study the process of collaboration as closely as possible, she confined herself to pairs.

37 Theo van Doesburg painting the model of Maison Particulière in the studio in Paris, 1923
Het Nieuwe Instituut, Rotterdam

Bos distinguished several forms of collective work, of which 'active collaboration' was the most intensive and the most effective. This was characterized by a frank, lively and stimulating exchange of ideas. In this shared thought process, the participants are so intellectually stimulated that their individual performances improve markedly. Active collaboration, Bos observed, leads to better results than individual work, because the collective situation is especially good at mobilizing the factors that are crucial to every productive work process: initiative, critical capacity and concentration. The one condition is a practical and businesslike attitude that makes the work itself the first priority. This positive mindset increases the spiritual activity, neutralizes obstructive or disruptive influences and ensures a common goal and a work atmosphere in which individual differences dissolve.[13]

## Collaborative duos

Publications like that of Bos signalled the beginning of a growing stream of behavioural science studies of social dynamics and collaboration.[14] Gradually, experimental laboratory studies were supplemented with qualitative research into collaborative arrangements in real-life situations, which meant taking more account of the complexity and rich dynamics of group processes; creativity was not just a psychological phenomenon, but a social and cultural one as well. Some sixty years after Bos, the

American psychologist Vera John-Steiner explored the theme of collaborating duos from a broader perspective in *Creative Collaboration* (2000).[15] Her starting point was the contention that a joint exploration of ideas is crucial for a renewal of artistic or intellectual insights. John-Steiner studied the activities of thirteen famous duos from the worlds of the visual arts, music, dance, literature and science. She, too, distinguished several forms of collaboration, the highest of which in her view was the

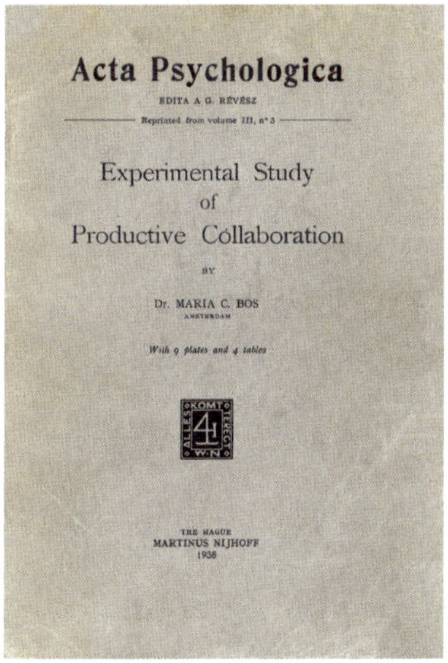


38 Maria Bos, 'Experimental Study of Productive Collaboration', 1937 (reprint 1938)

'integrative' form. This demanded dedication and was based on a profound sense of commitment. The partners challenged one another, gave careful consideration to one another's contributions, learned from one another and in so doing surpassed their usual way of learning, working and creating. Through this intense form of collaboration they together constructed new creative syntheses, and transformed both the subject matter and themselves.

However different in origin and setup, the studies by Bos and John-Steiner are both enlightening in this context, because they cast Van Eesteren's ideas about the benefits of collaboration into sharper relief. Not only do they analyse different gradations of collectivity and their effects, but they also demonstrate that the most important condition for collaboration lies in the participants' state of mind. When we put the descriptions by Bos and Van Eesteren side by side, it is evident that the latter must have experienced his work with Van Doesburg on the Maison d'Artiste as a form of 'active' collaboration; the result was not the mere sum of both their contributions, but a creative synthesis, or in Van Eesteren's own words, a 'new entity'. Although their alliance was short-lived, Van Eesteren and Van Doesburg also achieved the highest level of collaboration as analysed by John-Steiner. In a way the Dutch duo surpassed Pablo Picasso (1881–1973) and Georges Braque (1882–1963), whose joint 'creation' of cubism was hailed by John-Steiner as the most striking example of integrative collaboration. The two painters had been close friends since 1907 and for seven years worked very closely together, resulting in marked thematic and stylistic similarities in their work. But however intensive their contact, they both continued to work on their own and they did not make any co-productions they could both sign. By contrast, Van Eesteren and Van Doesburg, based on the complementarity of painter and architect, achieved in the space of just a few months a unique form of integrative collaboration that resulted in a joint design for the Maison d'Artiste that they did in fact both put their name to. The downside of this condensed joint creativity was its brevity. After the Paris exhibition, misunderstandings and copyright issues between Van Eesteren and Van Doesburg led to mutual mistrust, rendering further collaboration impossible.

## Continual interaction

Van Eesteren nevertheless drew considerable inspiration from the 'collective construction' process with Van Doesburg. In 1924 he proffered it as a model when discussing a possible collaboration with his friend Knut Lønberg-Holm (1895–1972), a Danish architect who had departed for the United States in 1923. According to Van Eesteren, the Paris models showed what results could be achieved in this way, although in this case it had only involved an architect and a painter. 'This collaboration of kindred spirits needs to be further expanded in order to achieve something worthwhile in practice,' he wrote to Lønberg-Holm in 1924.[16] For various reasons nothing came of this plan, but Van Eesteren continued to work as part of a team; 'I've become anonymous on its account,' he once wrote to the architect Jaap Bakema (1914–1981).[17] He did place high demands on

11 Bos 1937.
12 Bos mentions Shaw; see: Bos 1937, p. 318.
13 See also Somer 2007, pp. 76–77.
14 John-Steiner 2003.
15 John-Steiner 2000.
16 'Man sollte diese Zusammenarbeit gleich eingestellter Geister noch weiter ausbreiten müssen, um practisch Schönes leisten zu können.' Letter from C. van Eesteren to K. Lønberg-Holm, 19 September 1924. Quoted in Bock 2001, p. 328.

mutual conduct and selected potential partners carefully, based on character and disposition. Van Eesteren was firmly convinced that only a collective work method could lead to the emergence of a shared contemporary view of the living environment that had universal validity. He held to his fundamental conviction that a joint effort would lead to the realization of the avant-garde pursuit of a synthesis of life and art. For him collaboration was not just a means, but also a goal: the form of existence of the creative individual.[18]

It was this attitude to life that Van Eesteren brought to his work as urban designer, including in official cooperative ventures where it was necessary to forge a synthesis of disparate social sectional interests by way of consultation. From 1929 onwards he was employed as architect-town planner in Amsterdam's town planning department, where he worked on the Algemeen Uitbreidingsplan (General Extension Plan, AUP for short).[19] One of the top council officials, the Director of Public Works W.A. de Graaf, regarded town planning as a pre-eminently collective affair that called for an 'organic' amalgamation of all elements and 'amicable teamwork by all involved'.[20] Van Eesteren was enthusiastic about this working method. He found the experience of developing a spatial master plan through the active collaboration of individuals and groups, based on a common goal, stimulating and productive. The pursuit of societal consensus gave the collaboration concrete social and political significance, which crystallized in the urban development plan for Amsterdam.

Van Eesteren brought this experience to an even bigger collective project, the planning and design of the southern IJsselmeer Polders. From 1942 onwards, he would devote his energy to this for almost a quarter of a century.[21] His objective was a spatially and aesthetically satisfying solution of a complex issue, that the responsible agencies had initially regarded as a primarily technical task. Van Eesteren was convinced that in a twentieth-century rationalized landscape, function and beauty could go hand in hand. Aware of the relativeness of the designer's role in this, he felt that the designer should fundamentally derive his relevance from the collective of which he was part. He could only realize his ideas 'in close, daily collaboration' with the other experts involved. 'Continual exchange is the condition for success,' Van Eesteren wrote. 'All the while remaining focused on the entirety of the man-made environment, woods, settlements, waterways, roads, dikes, residual lakes, connection with the old land, the polder as part of the region, etc.'[22] Confrontations with the limits of collectivity and personal disappointments were inevitable, but Van Eesteren regarded them as the consequences of his fundamental decision to seek collaboration within the bureaucracy as well. In that respect he differed from someone like the architect J.J.P. Oud (1890–1963), who turned his back on teamwork in architecture after the Second World War, because he believed that it had an adverse effect on the expressive power of the architecture.[23]

## Spiritual diffusion

It was above all in the previously mentioned CIAM that Van Eesteren propagated and practised the principle of collectivity with unmatched zeal. From the moment he became chairman in 1930, he strove to organize this international association of modern architects into a tight-knit cooperative that, thanks to the active involvement of all members, would surely arrive at new insights [fig. 39]. He regarded as crucial mutual friendship, support and trust – the same notions that Behne had put forward in 1919 as preconditions for international collaboration.[24] Van Eesteren believed that the members themselves, through mutual criticism and open discussion, should as a team become a prototype of the ideal new society.[25] Within CIAM he and secretary Giedion for years formed a duality. In the 1930s in particular they worked harmoniously and intensively together, as witnessed by the hundreds of preserved letters that had flown back and forth between the two men.[26] After Giedion's death in 1968, Van Eesteren looked back on their partnership: he and Giedion had formed 'a lively spiritual unit'; between them, based on mutual understanding, there was 'spiritual permeation' such that both discovered 'something new – and previously unsuspected'. He felt that they had succeeded in passing on this principle to CIAM: 'as long as CIAM experienced this kind of spiritual permeation, they were creative and productive. They were unexpected, dazzlingly new because of it.'[27] Mutatis mutandis, this sounds almost literally like his description of the collaboration with Van Doesburg 45 years earlier. Whether it concerned an artwork, an urban development plan or a cooperative organization like CIAM, what mattered for Van Eesteren was its conception in a 'collective construction' as a prefiguration of a society in which art and life would be integrated.

39 From l to r: S. Giedion, C. van Eesteren, K. Moser, W. Gropius and V. Bourgeois during the CIAM delegates' meeting in Amsterdam, June 1935
Het Nieuwe Instituut, Rotterdam

17 Letter from C. van Eesteren to J.B. Bakema, 31 March 1957. Quoted in Bock 1993, p. 9.

18 Bock, Van Rossem and Somer 2001, p. 329.

19 Van Rossem 1993.

20 Bock 1993, p. 8.

21 Hemel 1994.

22 Hemel 1994.

23 Broekhuizen 2000, pp. 17–20.

24 C. van Eesteren, manuscript of opening address at sixth CIAM Congress, Bridgwater 1947, p. 4; HNI, BODE.

25 Letter from C. van Eesteren to E. Rogers, 30 April 1952; HNI, Van Eesteren archive.

26 The bulk of the correspondence between Van Eesteren and Giedion is held in ETH Zurich, GTA archive and Het Nieuwe Instituut, Rotterdam, Van Eesteren archive. See Somer 2007.

27 Letter from C. van Eesteren to C. Welcker, 16 June 1968; HNI, Van Eesteren archive. Quotations in German: 'eine lebendige geistige Einheit … spirituelle Durchdringung … etwas neues – und vorher nicht bewusstes … solange die CIAM diese Art der geistige Durchdringung erlebten waren sie schöpferisch und produktiv. Unerwartet, sprudelisch neu waren sie dadurch.'

40 Theo van Doesburg and Cornelis van Eesteren, retouching photos of model of Maison d'Artiste, c. 1924. Background cut out, stuck on and coloured white, so that the model appears omni-directional and floating.
RKD – Netherlands Institute for Art History, The Hague

Dolf Broekhuizen

# Interpreting the Maison d'Artiste Historiography of a design

## The reception of a momentous design

The Maison d'Artiste occupies a fascinating place in the history of De Stijl. The initial press reactions presented the project, together with the two other Paris models, as the biggest surprise of the De Stijl exhibition in Galerie L'Effort Moderne in 1923. The reviewers' comments were not uniformly laudatory, however. Surprise, amazement and disapproval alternated regarding the idiosyncratic character of the construction, which appeared to defy the laws of gravity [fig. 40]. The seemingly free-floating planes looked decidedly impracticable. The design immediately secured a crucial position in the debate about architecture as a manifesto of De Stijl. In the years that followed, this impression gradually became more nuanced as more and more became known about Van Doesburg and Van Eesteren's individual oeuvres and about the Modern Movement. This chapter sheds light on the main themes of the many interpretations and analyses that have been published about the Maison d'Artiste: the position the project occupied in Van Doesburg and Van Eesteren's architectural theory, the Maison d'Artiste as part of De Stijl, and Maison d'Artiste's contribution to architectural history.

## Architectural theory

One of the key ideas underlying Maison d'Artiste is what Van Eesteren and Van Doesburg regarded as the dynamic conception of space. In order to achieve that dynamism, collaboration between painter and architect was important, as were the composition of space, planes and colours. The idea was that the impressions an individual experienced as a result of the design of total architecture, would alter their frame of mind. To underpin the dynamic conception of space, the artists drew inspiration from new scientific ideas, such as colour theory, but more especially mathematics.[1] The concept of the fourth dimension, which was popular in the first two decades of the twentieth century, came to Van Doesburg's attention around 1917 via the French cubists and the mathematicians M. Schoenmaekers and Henri Poincaré.[2] A few years later, Van Doesburg and Van Eesteren themselves propounded this theoretical concept, which holds that movement through space influences the ultimate perception of the total living environment, in their joint manifesto 'Vers une construction collective' (1923), which was written especially for the Rosenberg exhibition.[3] There Van Eesteren and Van Doesburg defined the analysis of 'space and time' as part of the new architecture. In 'Tot een beeldende architectuur' (1924), which was published in *De Stijl*, and 'De nieuwe architectuur', published in the *Bouwkundig Weekblad*, Van Doesburg elaborated on this idea.[4]

### Van Eesteren's 'activating houses'

The earliest explanations Van Eesteren gave of the Paris models, from 1923 onwards, mention the time–space element. Architectural historian Manfred Bock has detected the influence of Van Doesburg in these particular texts. According to Bock, the three models were an exception in Van Eesteren's body of work, and his thinking in this period was strongly influenced by Van Doesburg. Although Van Eesteren himself 'did not or would not see' that exceptionality, Bock is in no doubt that the intensive contact with Van Doesburg in 1923 amounted to 'an intellectual earthquake that disrupted and perhaps enriched his thinking.'[5] According to Bock, Van Eesteren blended his more functional approach with Van Doesburg's views. This becomes apparent, for example, in the rather impenetrable-sounding explanations Van Eesteren wrote at this time: 'Space is expansion and

1 Matthias Noell recently published a fascinating study of Van Doesburg's studio-house in Meudon. It contains a detailed chapter on the colour with copious references: Noell 2011, pp. 119–151.

2 Blotkamp 1982, p. 39.

3 Van Doesburg and Van Eesteren 1924.

4 Van Doesburg 1924a; Van Doesburg 1924b.

5 Bock 2001, p. 128.

compression with *n* dimensions. Since space is a three-dimensional concept, we need to use a different word: infinity. Architecture [is] an infinity defined by means of space in space.' In later writings Van Eesteren confined himself to 'his usual functional, businesslike and thoroughly human approach'.[6] A few years after the exhibition, probably in 1925, by which time Van Eesteren had acquired more detachment and was writing for a publication about the domestic interior, he referred more

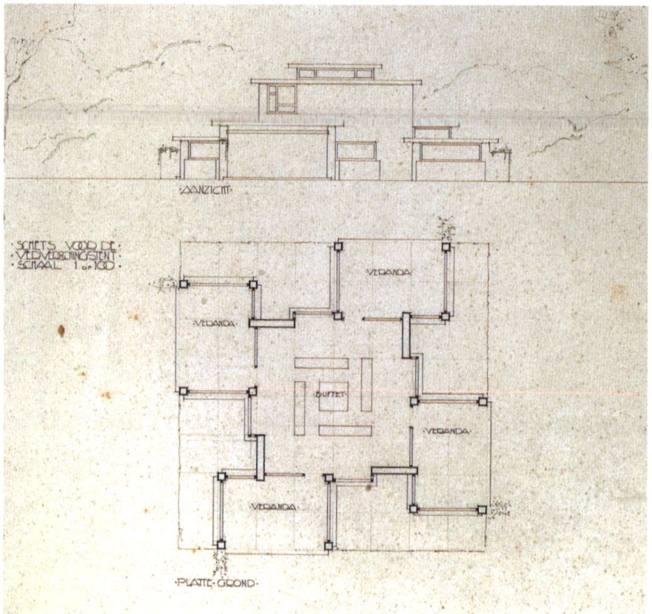


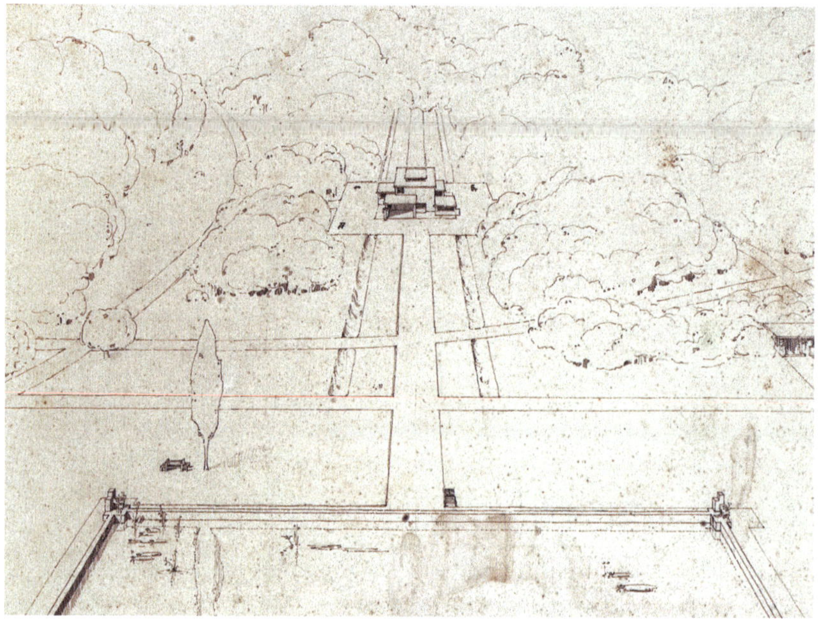

41 Jan Wils, Central point in the IJ-Bosch in Amsterdam, 1917-1918, floor plan and elevation of refreshment stand, detail of presentation drawing for competition design. Het Nieuwe Instituut, Rotterdam

42 Jan Wils, Central point in the IJ-Bosch in Amsterdam, 1917-1918, refreshment stand, detail of presentation drawing for competition design. Het Nieuwe Instituut, Rotterdam

43 Theo van Doesburg, design drawing refreshment kiosk, c. 1922. Van Doesburg's drawing looks to be based on Wils's design for a refreshment stand from 1917-1918. Het Nieuwe Instituut, Rotterdam

44 Theo van Doesburg, design drawing refreshment kiosk, c. 1922. Volumetric study, used by Doesburg for his 'basic elements'. Het Nieuwe Instituut, Rotterdam

matter-of-factly to the features of the Paris models.[7] In these descriptions of the Maison Particulière and the Maison d'Artiste he focused on the functional aspects and the associated experience of the space: 'The last design (artist's house) represents the strongest attempt to combine all the domestic functions and needs as freely and loosely as possible,' Van Eesteren wrote. 'One could speak of activating houses with opportunities everywhere for genuine rest and relaxation.'[8]

### Van Doesburg's elementary expressive means

For an understanding of Van Doesburg's conception of space immediately before the creation of the Paris models, his publications, sketches and letters are illuminating. In 1922, probably in connection with the De Stijl course and lectures he was giving in Weimar, Van Doesburg worked on his theory of the 'basic elements': elementary means which enable painting, sculpture and architecture to merge in a single harmonious whole. He no longer made any distinction between architecture as a subordinate, applied art tied to function and construction, and a separate art of painting and sculpture; instead there is an expressive architecture. Such a view made autonomous painting and sculpture redundant as they were completely merged with the new architecture: the expressive means of painting (colour) and sculpture (plasticity) came together in architecture. In the basic elements, Van Doesburg reduced painting to smooth colour planes in the three primary colours red, blue and yellow, and the three non-colours black, grey and white. These colours, having been organically incorporated into architecture, serve to render visible the 'relations in time and space'. The way the painter visualized the expressive means for sculpture and architecture is interesting in this context because Van Doesburg had borrowed them from a design by the architect Jan Wils, with whom he had collaborated briefly in a De Stijl context in 1917–1918 on, among other things, the fountain design for Leeuwarden. In 1922 he approached Wils once again in relation to the design of the Maison Rosenberg, but nothing came of that.

There has been no previous mention of the fact that in developing these plastic and spatial basic elements, Van Doesburg had reworked a 1918 competition design by Jan Wils [figs. 41, 42].[9] In 1922, Van Doesburg used Wils's unrealized design for a 'refreshment stand' as the basis for the illustrations accompanying his argument by abstracting the form into simple rectangular masses [figs. 43, 44]. This represented his basic architectural elements and then, by rotating the whole thing ninety degrees, he represented the basic elements of sculpture [fig. 45]. The source of the tall central cube, surrounded by four shorter cubes in a rotating movement is patently obvious from the two surviving design sketches by Van Doesburg, dated 1922.[10] That source is interesting, because it is another instance of Van Doesburg developing his theory in interaction with an architect,

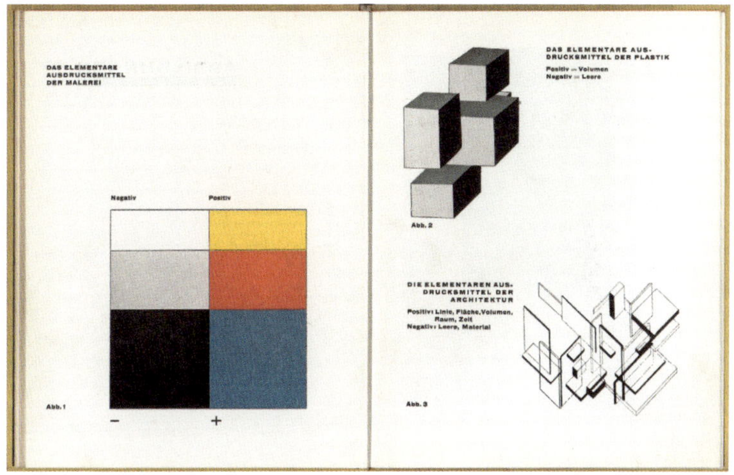


45 Theo van Doesburg, 'basic elements' of painting (left), sculpture and architecture (right), 1923. Pictured in Theo van Doesburg, *Grundbegriffe der neuen gestaltenden Kunst* (*Bauhausbuch* 6), 1925
RKD – Netherlands Institute for Art History, The Hague

in this case not in an actual collaboration, but retrospectively in the form of an independent reworking of an existing design.[11] In the central tall volume surrounded by an arrangement of discrete smaller volumes, it is not difficult to detect the basic form of the Maison d'Artiste.

6 HNI EEST 3.356, quoted in Bock 2001, p. 128.

7 This text was eventually published in 1931 in the series *Onze woning en haar inrichting*, but was written earlier: Van Eesteren 1931.

8 [C. van Eesteren], 'De beide hierbij afgebeelde woonhuizen...' 'Beide hierbij afgebeelde ontwerpen ...', two manuscript versions, undated [1925-1931], HNI EEST 3.358-1; see also quotations in Bock 2001, pp. 131-132.

9 J. Wils, 'Ontwerp voor een Centraalpunt in het Y-bosch te Amsterdam. Schets voor de verversingstent', 1918, HNI WILS 1534; De Meijer 1918; interesting in relation to this design is Wils's article about nature and culture, and symmetry and asymmetry in De Stijl: Wils 1918.

10 Van Straaten 1988, p. 104.

11 Hoek et al. 2000, cat. no. 674 I-III.

**Counter-constructions and tesseract**

In later texts Van Doesburg and Van Eesteren were fond of linking the key constituent of the Maison d'Artiste, the dynamic concept of space, to a time–space theory that was popular among artists at that time. The photographs of the models and the counter-constructions (also known as 'architectural analyses') drawn in 1923 and later, give expression to the idea that elements such as colour, surface and space are experienced in relation to one another and alter the observer's awareness through the combined impression they evoke as the observer moves through the building. Although only one incomplete counter-construction of the Maison d'Artiste is known, in which Van Doesburg tried out the colours, several completed counter-constructions of the Maison Particulière have survived, which are demonstrations of the time–space theory. The free-floating planes in the axonometric projection, in which the building is drawn at an angle of 45 degrees, underscore that endeavour. The importance of the centripetal and centrifugal directions is evident from the drawings relating to expressive means, which Van Doesburg used to illustrate his article in *Architectura* (1923) [fig. 46].

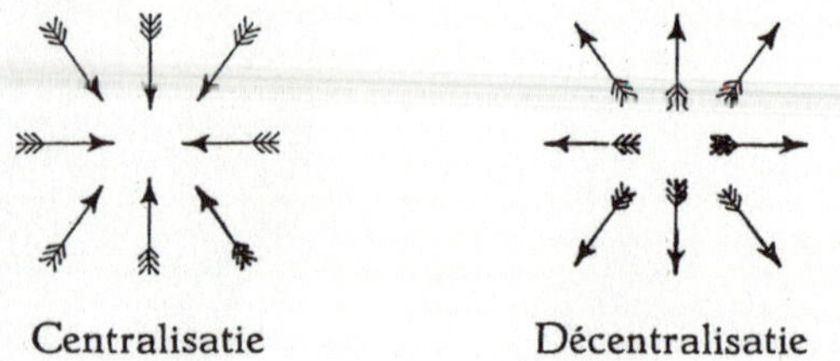


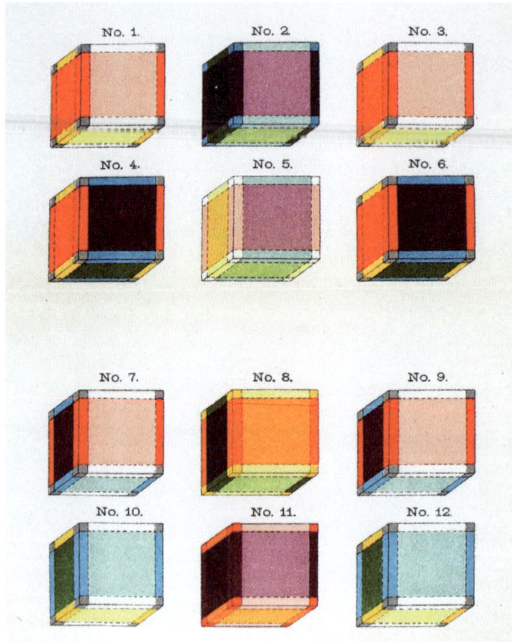


46 Theo van Doesburg, 'Centralization, decentralization' illustration in 'Voorwaarden tot een nieuwe architectuur' ('Pre-conditions for a new architecture'), *Architectura* 1923.

47 Charles Howard Hinton, tesseract studies, in: *The Fourth Dimension*, 1904

In 1924 and 1925, Van Doesburg utilized another mathematical idea relating to the fourth dimension in his theory.[12] From 1924 onwards, Van Doesburg used the mathematical figure of the unfolded hypercube (known then as a tesseract), which depicts the fourth dimension, in his work. The English mathematician Charles Howard Hinton (1853–1907), who developed the concept, depicted the fourth dimension in his 1904 book, even though the concept is in fact impossible to visualize [fig. 47].[13]

In the figure of the tesseract, a cube moves through a three-dimensional space in such a way that the fourth dimension becomes visible. Time plays a role in this. Van Doesburg drew these figures, which he labelled 'schematic representation of a tesseract', as part of the theoretical and expressive research he carried out from 1924 onwards (fig. 48). He also referred to the tesseract in his articles in support of his argument. He not only wrote about it in the construction trade journals *Bouwkundig Weekblad* and *Het Bouwbedrijf*, but also corresponded about it with Hannah Höch and László Moholy-Nagy.[14] It turned out that the latter, as a teacher at the Bauhaus, was in touch with the celebrated mathematician Albert Einstein on the matter, and in July 1924 he reported on this in his letters to Van Doesburg.[15]

### Reactions

Right from the beginning, it was not only Van Doesburg and Van Eesteren who made a connection between the Maison d'Artiste and the dynamic spatial concept; critics, the professional press and Mondrian all recognized the Maison d'Artiste as the embodiment of a theory.[16] In 1923 and 1924, both the French and Dutch press construed the models in the Paris exhibition as demonstrations of an architectural concept based on a design theory. De Stijl's fifth manifesto, 'Vers une construction collective' (1923), which Van Doesburg had had printed in pamphlet form for the exhibition, would have been regarded as an explanation of that theory, but other writings and opinions, by Mondrian for example, were well-known at the time and would also have contributed to this interpretation. Although French and Dutch reviewers were impressed by the theoretical calibre, they immediately started to question the technical feasibility and practical utility of the architectural design.[17]

In later considerations, that aspect of feasibility and theoretical development cropped up time and again. There has been extensive research into the authorship of the models, and the way Van Doesburg and Van Eesteren collaborated, with researchers emphasizing different aspects and making different connections. In the 1960s, Jean Leering (1968) and Joost Baljeu (1968, 1974) placed considerable emphasis on the fourth dimension, and tried to render it experienceable or understandable in exhibitions. In the 1980s researchers pointed out that it was not until 1924 that Van Doesburg started applying the tesseract to his theories in letters and publications, in other words, after the creation of the Maison d'Artiste. In his doctoral thesis (1988), art historian Evert van Straaten called the tesseract drawings of 1924–1925 a retrospective justification of the Maison d'Artiste by Van Doesburg.[18] He also made a connection with a cinematic point of view in which the experience of time and the abandonment of the static play a role, and he referred to contacts Van Doesburg had with the German painter and filmmaker Hans Richter (1888–1976) in the years

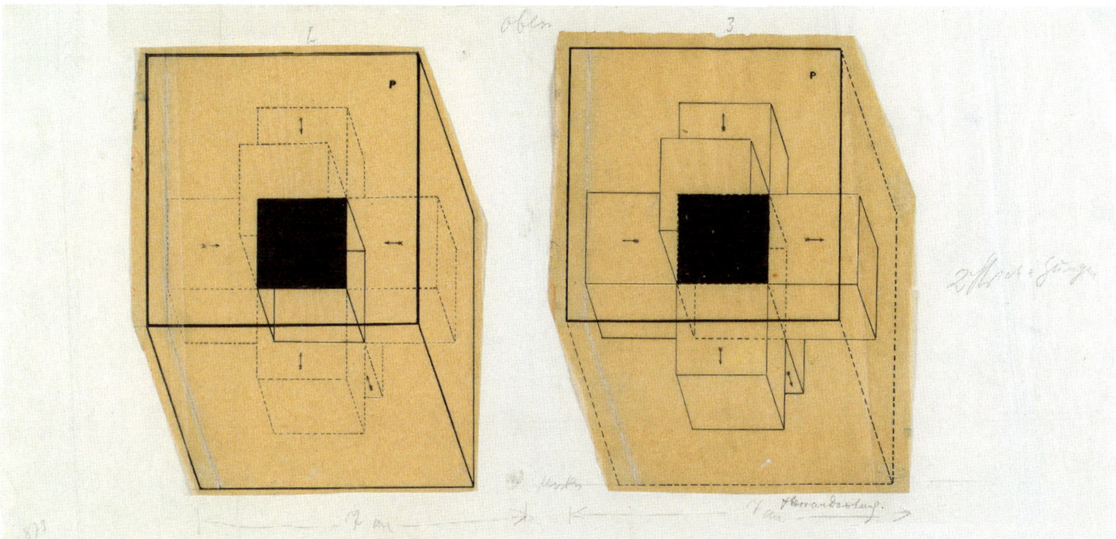

48 Theo van Doesburg, diagram of a tesseract, 1924-1925. Arrows pointing inwards and outwards. Het Nieuwe Instituut, Rotterdam

12 Van Straaten 1988, pp. 190–195; Bock 2001, p. 128.

13 Gasten 1978; Vink 1990; cf.: Goddijn 2000.

14 Van Doesburg 1924b; Boekraad 1986, p. 85.

15 See Galison et al. 2006, p. 324, note 33; the letter is included in Boekraad 1983a, p. 109.

16 For Mondrian's critical reaction: anonymous, 17 October 1924; see also: Hanssen 2015, p. 212.

17 Anonymous 1923a, Anonymous 1923b, Mesnil 1923, Rambosson 1923, Veissière 1923. For an analysis, see Bois 1983, pp. 104-107.

18 Van Straaten 1988, pp. 190-191; see also Bock 1996, p. 266 and Bock 2001, p. 178.

1921–1925. In 2001, in a detailed study of the three Paris projects of Van Eesteren and Van Doesburg, the architectural historian Manfred Bock emphasized the conceptual significance of the design – the spatial concept that underpinned it – and explored the connection with other projects.[19] These included housing projects from the same period, such as Huis van Zessen by both men in Kinderdijk (1923) [fig. 49], the 'bi-carré' home (Groutars House, 1924) by Van Doesburg, and Van Doesburg's colour design for the flower room in Villa Noailles (1924–1925) [fig. 50], as well as connections with projects by other architects.

Despite these thoroughgoing studies, new facts continue to surface. The spatial quality and the fourth dimension continue to fascinate researchers, as witnessed by the 2010 study by Marek Wieczorek, who demonstrated that Van Doesburg had referred to publications about the tesseract as early as 1918, in letters to Georges Vantongerloo. He showed that Van Doesburg may well have been inspired by the writings of the French mathematician and physicist Maurice Boucher, who published an article on the new gravitational theories in 1903.[20]

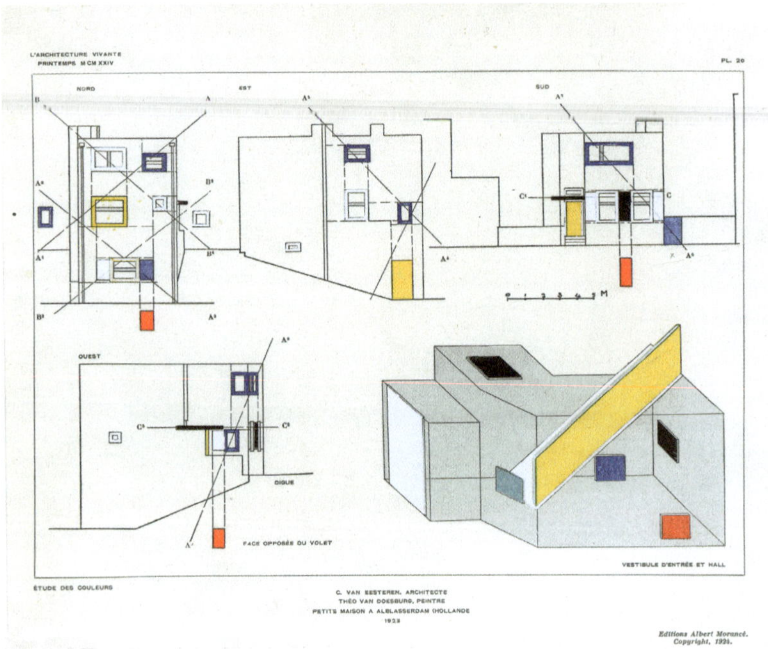


49 Cornelis van Eesteren and Theo van Doesburg,
Huis van Zessen, Kinderdijk (Alblasserdam) 1923.
Four elevations with colour scheme and counter-construction for the vestibule and staircase (bottom right).
Het Nieuwe Instituut, Rotterdam

50 Theo van Doesburg, colour design for the flower room in Villa Noailles, Hyères, 1924-1925.
Four walls (folded out) and the ceiling in the middle.
Van Abbemuseum, Eindhoven /
photo Peter Cox, Eindhoven

## Part of De Stijl

In art-historical texts about the Maison d'Artiste great importance is attached to the Paris De Stijl exhibition in 1923 because that event saw the birth of this project and the two other designs by Van Doesburg and Van Eesteren, which later became known as the three 'Paris models'. In fact, without the exhibition the models would not have existed (in that form) since they were made especially for the event. As such, the exhibition in the renowned art gallery contributed to De Stijl's international reputation. Maison Particulière and Maison d'Artiste in particular went on to become iconic works. Maison Rosenberg gave the impression of being easier to build because the construction, with walls that extended over several storeys, was less experimental.

The accompanying 'image', which was to play such an important role for the designers in the dissemination of their ideas, was not available in time for the exhibition. Van Doesburg and Van Eesteren were dissatisfied with the black-and-white photographs they had commissioned because the maquettes had been photographed complete with stand. They were also very brightly lit so that 'all the model's tiny defects' had been captured, as Van Doesburg wrote to Van Eesteren.[21] Owing to the lack of acceptable photographs, the planned publication had to be postponed. It was a year before satisfactory photographs were finally published. The artists resolved the problem by retouching the photos [figs. 52, 53]. The French magazine *L'Architecture vivante* (1925) was the first to publish the Maison Particulière in colour, together with the two other Paris designs [fig. 51].[22]

51 Theo van Doesburg and Cornelis van Eesteren, Colour studies of Maison Particulière. Elevations and axonometric. Plate 5 in: *'Architecture vivante*, 1925, one of the earliest publications of the design in colour. Het Nieuwe Instituut, Rotterdam

The counter-constructions of the designs appeared later on in exhibition posters and on the covers of books about De Stijl.

In the reviews that appeared in the French and Dutch press immediately after the opening of the Rosenberg exhibition, critics regarded the Maison d'Artiste as a characteristic example of De Stijl architecture. This collaborative project of Van Doesburg and Van Eesteren was seen as a manifestation of De Stijl as a movement.[23] The architecture critic for the *Rotterdamsche Courant* described the architecture as three-dimensional Mondrians: cubic volumes were stacked and 'assembled into paintings in the manner of Mondrian'.[24] In these early articles, De Stijl was presented as a movement whose primary goal was a synthesis of the arts and which shared a modern vocabulary drawn mainly from the visual arts. Artists and architects worked together to create an abstract living environment, stripped of historical references and purified down to primary colours, rectangular planes and asymmetrical spatial compositions. Since the 1980s, however, art historians have pointed to the fact that the movement's magazine could scarcely be said to present coherent ideas or a common goal propagated by the artists.[25] The collective manifestos, for example, were drafted or signed by a variety of artists. It was mainly Van Doesburg who propagated the image of a group, of which the exhibition 'Les Architectes du Groupe "de Styl"' and the manifesto that Van Doesburg hastily had printed, were confirmation.[26]

After the Second World War there was renewed interest in De Stijl. In the lead-up to the exhibitions on De Stijl in Amsterdam's Stedelijk Museum in 1951 and in the Museum of Modern Art in New York in 1952, former De Stijl members Rietveld, Van Eesteren and J.J.P. Oud discussed what exactly De Stijl had been and which image of De Stijl should be propagated at exhibitions. The two De Stijl exhibitions marked the beginning of the debate as to whether De Stijl should be regarded first and foremost as an unfinished, never realized utopia, or as an avant-garde movement in Dutch cultural history which came to an end with the death of its leading light, Van Doesburg, in 1931. Both in the choice of exhibition material and in the editing of the catalogues, those involved disagreed over whether to emphasize collectivity or individuality. Another question that arose in the course of this discussion,

**19** Bock 2001, pp. 151–153; see also Somer's contribution (Chapter 6).

**20** Wieczorek 2010 (p. 73) mentions the letter from T. van Doesburg to G. Vantongerloo of 7 June 1918. He refers to M. Boucher, *Essay sur l'hyperespace. Le temps, la matière, et l'énergie*, Paris 1903.

**21** Letter from T. van Doesburg to C. van Eesteren, 23 November 1923, HNI EEST 3.363.

**22** Badovici 1925, plates 2-7; see also Migayrou 2010, pp. 98-100, 102.

**23** For an analysis of reactions in the Dutch and French press: Bois 1983, pp. 104–107.

**24** Anonymous 19 October 1923.

**25** See for example Polano 1982, p. 88 and Troy 1982, p. 168.

**26** For the manifesto see Ottevanger 2008, p. 441.

was the desirability of recreating the non-extant maquettes.[27]

Van Eesteren and Rietveld in particular adopted very decided positions regarding making new models and objects for the exhibitions. For the De Stijl exhibition in the Stedelijk Museum in Amsterdam, Rietveld had proposed arranging an entire room with new models that would together give an impression of De Stijl as a collective endeavour and an unfinished utopia.[28] In suggesting that both the models and the reliefs of floor plans as well as the entire room should be painted white, Rietveld's intention was to accentuate the non-realistic nature of the projects [fig. 54].[29] Oud, too, was in favour of remaking the models, but for a very different reason. He saw it as an opportunity to emphasize individual contributions. He included in the exhibition a model of his design for Villa Johnson (1930–1931) made in 1951.

Right from the start, Van Eesteren was dismissive of Rietveld's proposal for a white room. He regarded the original (non-extant) objects from 1923 as artworks – unique and irreplaceable – and he rejected any and every derivative, such as a later reconstruction, as imitation. He thought that the white room was more appropriate to an advertising campaign with 'exhibitor stands' than a historical exhibition about art. What was more, the original models had been executed in colour, and Rietveld wanted to dispense with reconstructing that colour. In a letter to the director of the Stedelijk Museum, Willem Sandberg, Van Eesteren wrote that because the models 'have acquired a personal character, through the way they came into being and the painting, they are comparable to a painting and are consequently "einmalig"' (unique).[30] As a result of Van Eesteren's stance, the idea of a white room did not in the end go ahead.[31]

52, 53 Glass negative of the model of Maison Particulière retouched by Theo van Doesburg, c. 1924. The stand has been painted out. Het Nieuwe Instituut, Rotterdam

The editing of the catalogue for the De Stijl exhibition in the Stedelijk Museum was another source of discussion [fig. 55]. The initial idea was to publish original texts dating from the period 1917–1931. The selection of certain texts could be used to emphasize the theoretical contribution of, say Mondrian, or Van Doesburg's propagandistic activities.[32] In the catalogue of the De Stijl exhibition held the following year in the MoMA in

New York, the curators, Philip Johnson and Alfred Barr, presented De Stijl as a pre-war avant-garde movement which had made a significant contribution to aesthetic renewal (fig. 56).[33] In so doing, they deviated from the likes of the Italian Bruno Zevi, who was almost simultaneously laying the stress on De Stijl as a movement intent on effecting social change.[34] These differing views made it clear that Van Doesburg had defined De Stijl in three different ways and had also used those definitions simultaneously. In the 1980s, the art historian Yve-Alain Bois brought clarity to the representation of De Stijl by pointing to the three definitions of De Stijl: *De Stijl* as *magazine* with a clear beginning and end (1917–1931), De Stijl as a *group* of artists who published articles in the magazine, and De Stijl as an *idea* that the members of the group shared.[35]

During the 1960s, '70s and '80s, more became known about De Stijl and the individual oeuvres of its members, thanks to

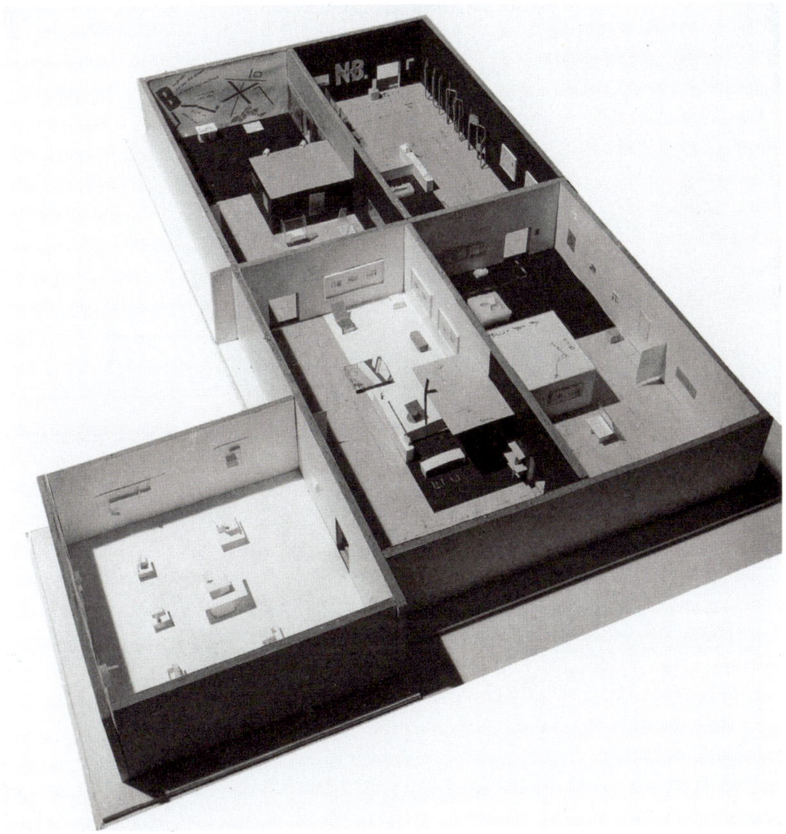

54 Gerrit Rietveld, model for the layout of the 'De Stijl' exhibition, Stedelijk Museum Amsterdam, 1951. Left in the foreground, the unrealized 'white room' with reconstructions of designs on tables and against the wall.
Rietveld Schröder archive / Centraal Museum, Utrecht

55 Cover of the *De Stijl* exhibition catalogue, Stedelijk Museum Amsterdam, 1951 (graphic design Willem Sandberg).
An axonometric of Maison Particulière was chosen as main image for the De Stijl event.

**27** In 1947, Philip Johnson suggested having the three Paris models made by architecture students. Notes C. van Eesteren, 15 May 1947, HNI EEST 10.760. See also Broekhuizen 2000, p. 289.

**28** Letter from G.T. Rietveld to J.J.P. Oud, 5 May 1951, HNI OUDJ; Broekhuizen 2000, pp. 285–291; Van Moorsel 2000, pp. 239–245.

**29** During the setting up of the New York exhibition, Rietveld said to the curator Philip Johnson: 'One cannot really build in De Stijl'. Letter from P.C. Johnson to J.J.P. Oud, 19 December 1952, HNI OUDJ C27; see also Broekhuizen 2000, p. 289.

**30** Letter from C. van Eesteren to W.J.H.B. Sandberg, 2 July 1951, HNI EEST 10.760. See also Broekhuizen 2000, p. 289.

**31** Rietveld did however make a new model of the Maison Rosenberg (Hôtel Particulier) in 1951 especially for the exhibition (as he had also done in 1923), but it is unclear whether it was ever actually exhibited. Reproduced in Janssen White 2011, p. 165. For the design drawings of the 'De Stijl' exhibition: CMU, RSA 883; HNI BROZ 586; photographs in several archives inc. SMA and HNI RIET 783; for the activities of Sandberg and De Stijl 1951 see: Roodenburg-Schadd 2004, pp. 517-523.

**32** Van den Broek 1951.

**33** The MoMA catalogue includes Barr's article about De Stijl from *Cubism and Abstract Art* (1936): Johnson and Barr 1952, pp. 7–12.

**34** Zevi 1953. Zevi repeated his view in 1968 at the opening of the Van Doesburg exhibition: Zevi 1969; see Schumacher 2010, pp. 115–116.

**35** Bois 1985, p. 11.

independent research and the fact that archives were transferred to public institutions. Groundbreaking research by Hans Jaffé (1956) was still in large part based on a thorough analysis of numerous original articles in relation to the work. Later researchers, such as Jean Leering (1969), director of the Van Abbemuseum in Eindhoven, and the Dutch artist Joost Baljeu (1974), made more use of correspondence, giving rise to a more nuanced view of the ideas and projects, while debates, intentions and painting came to be regarded as equal to architecture because colour had been fully integrated with architecture instead of being applied. In that respect, Troy evaluated Van Doesburg's efforts quite differently from those of Mondrian who treated the walls of his studio as a painter's surface and regarded his autonomy as sacrosanct; Mondrian never collaborated with architects. In relation to the architecture projects carried out by the painters Huszár and Van Doesburg in the early 1920s, Troy wrote: 'Unlike

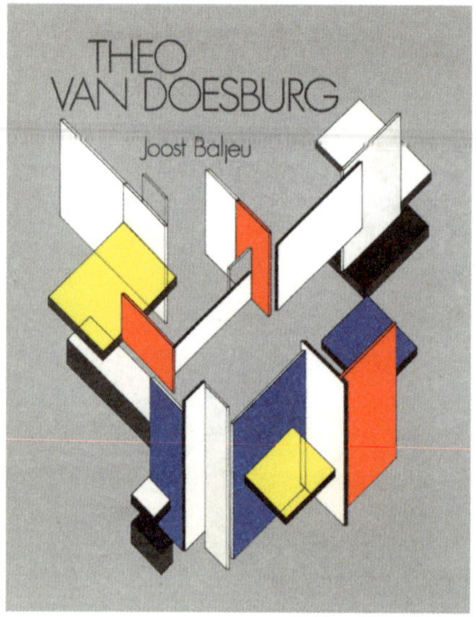


56 Cover of *De Stijl, The Museum of Modern Art Bulletin*, New York, 1952/1953. Publication accompanying the first historical exhibition about De Stijl in the MoMA in New York. A counter-construction of Maison Particulière was chosen for the cover. This counter-construction is in the MoMA collection (Edgar Kaufmann Jr. Fund)

57 Joost Baljeu, *'Theo van Doesburg'*, 1974 (graphic design M.L. Luxemburg). On the cover a counter-construction of Maison Particulière

differences of opinion also emerged [fig. 57]. In the early 1980s, the transfer of Van Doesburg's estate to the Dutch state triggered several exhibitions and publications about Van Doesburg's body of work in which new insights were presented. For these and later exhibitions, models of Maison Particulière and Maison d'Artiste were recreated (figs. 58, 59).[36] In the accompanying catalogues and other studies, the image of a coherent movement with shared principles and a common visual identity was undermined, and ample consideration was given to individual contributions and the discussions about collaborative projects.[37]

In this context it is illuminating to read the studies by the American art historian Nancy Troy, who pointed out in the 1980s that it is possible to distinguish several phases in what she regarded as the core of De Stijl, the collaboration between artist and architect. As she saw it, the Maison d'Artiste was emblematic of the pursuit of complete synthesis in the first half of the 1920s.[38] Collaborative projects in this period (c. 1921–1925) show that Mondrian, these painters produced designs in which color functioned to propel the viewer through space. Instead of using color to reinforce planes perceived individually and then fused in the mind of the viewer, their aim was to tap the dynamic potential of color by moving it across surfaces and compelling the viewer himself to move in order to experience space in terms of time in an abstract realm made possible by color.'

For their part, today's historians do not go so far as to deny that De Stijl was a movement. The more recent publications about De Stijl are dominated by what is known as the repudiation of 'the De Stijl myth', because they point to agreements *and* conflicts about ideas and designs. One important manifestation of this was the study group headed by professor of art history, Carel Blotkamp, who in *De beginjaren van De Stijl* (1982) took a monographic approach. Blotkamp focused more on the diversity of opinions rather than placing the emphasis on a single idea.[40] Other researchers related the works to contexts other than

De Stijl and to broader cultural trends, such as urban design, advertising, the history of furniture or political events.[41] In addition to greater focus on individual oeuvres, the works of less well-known artists were also subjected to critical scrutiny. Even the historiography of the historiography has been the subject of analysis, as evidenced by the 2014 study of the context of Jaffé's doctoral thesis.[42]

## Contribution to architectural history

The Maison d'Artiste's place in architectural history is closely connected with the historiography of what is called the Modern Movement. This encompasses the avant-garde tendencies and innovative endeavours in the early decades of the twentieth century, such as De Stijl and Nieuwe Zakelijkheid in the Netherlands, cubism and L'Esprit Nouveau in France, Neue Sachlichkeit and the Bauhaus in Germany and futurism and *razionalismo* in

58 Model of Maison d'Artiste, reconstruction by Tjaarda Mees, 1982. Executed in wood, silk-screen, Perspex, Plexiglas, 62 x 60 x 60 cm. Gemeentemuseum, The Hague

59 Model of Maison d'Artiste, produced by Victor Veldhuijzen van Zanten and Frans Postma, 2006. Perspex and Plexiglas, scale 1:50, c. 40 x 40 x 40 cm. Owned by B. Campbell, F. Postma and V. Veldhuijzen van Zanten.
Photo Fas Keuzenkamp

**36** The Haags Gemeentemuseum included the 1983 models in its collection. They were made to the same scale (1:50) as the original models, but the materials used, including wood, Plexiglas, Perspex and screen print, were quite different from the original materials: cardboard, mica and glass. Pictured in Warncke 1998, pp. 169, 172 and Janssen White 2011, p. 165.

**37** Polano 1982; Boekraad 1982.

**38** In the previous phase the painter and artist strove for collaboration, but architecture dominated because of the constraints of usability and functionality (1916–1921). And in the third phase, from the second half of the 1920s, artists and architects were once again convinced of their autonomy. Troy 1982, p. 176.

**39** Troy 1982, p. 182.

**40** Blotkamp 1982, p. ix.

**41** For the historiography of De Stijl: White 2003, pp. xii-xv; and Janssen and White 2011, pp. 10-14.

**42** See the unpublished thesis on Hans Jaffé: Samantha Hoekema, *De Stijl (1956) als reactie op De Stijl (1951). Een onderzoek naar het proefschrift van Hans Jaffé*, Master's thesis General Cultural Studies, University of Amsterdam, October 2014.

Italy. In the first instance, it was the propagandists of the Modern Movement who drew attention to the innovative nature of the Maison d'Artiste and the other two Paris models. The authors of these early publications drew a distinction between traditional and modern, and presented innovation as the consequence of the exclusive mentality of the avant-gardes, who because of this would go on to exert a putatively dominant influence on later designers. The American architecture historian Henry-Russell Hitchcock, writing in 1929, was one of the first to mention the importance of the Maison d'Artiste for the development of the new architecture. In an authoritative general history, he argued that De Stijl was the most important experimental movement in the Netherlands and he saw the three models as its most important manifestations. Hitchcock, who was mistaken about the design year, wrote: 'It was the models of 1922 for an artist's house and two other houses, one very large [Maison Rosenberg], which were the most interesting and also the most widely remarked.'[43]

Possibly the most influential work in the historiography of modern architecture was Sigfried Giedion's *Space, Time and Architecture* (1941), in which innovation was likewise related to artistic tendencies such as purism (France), constructivism (Soviet Union) and neoplasticism (Netherlands). In this publication Giedion described the Maison Particulière as a bolt from the blue: 'In 1923 van Doesburg, together with van Eesteren ... produced a house that is bolder than any other building executed during the period.'[44] He praised the spatial art of the Maison Particulière as Van Doesburg's pursuit of 'pure art', which he regarded as equal to that of Mondrian. Giedion even included an architectural analysis of the project in the chapter about the spatial concepts of the Baroque and Neoclassicism [fig. 60]. He presented the quest by several architects of the period to eliminate the separation between inside and outside, and the meticulous application of spatial relations as a basic element of architecture, as a 'modern' endeavour that had finally been accomplished in revolutionary fashion by Van Doesburg and Van Eesteren.[45]

In the ensuing years the canonical status of the Maison d'Artiste and the other Paris models as the most innovative De Stijl architecture would compete with the private house that Rietveld designed a year after the Paris exhibition for Truus Schröder in Utrecht. Although Van Doesburg himself featured the Rietveld-Schröder House (1924) in *De Stijl*, it was not until the 1950s that the house became exemplary for De Stijl architecture, thanks to the De Stijl exhibitions [fig. 61].[46] The first edition of Giedion's standard work made no mention at all of Rietveld's architecture. It was not until the 1956 edition that Giedion, who was highly regarded among architects and historians, recognized the importance of the Rietveld-Schröder House. Other works, such as Hitchcock's *Architecture. Nineteenth and Twentieth Centuries* (1958) and Benevolo's *Modern Architecture* (1960),

60 Theo van Doesburg, Cornelis van Eesteren, counter-construction depicting architecture's basic means of expression, (*Bauhausbuch* 1925), pictured in: S. Giedion, *Space, Time and Architecture. The Growth of a New Tradition*, 1941.
Het Nieuwe Instituut, Rotterdam

also drew a link between the design of the unrealized Paris model and the realized Utrecht house.[47] In so doing, historians happily noted that Rietveld had made the Maison Rosenberg maquette. It is typical of the 1980s that from then on the link was considerably played down and writers emphasized the individual and specific character of the designs within the various oeuvres.

In the 1980s and '90s the image of the avant-garde movements was further stripped of clichés. Architectural historians like David Watkin and V.M. Lampugnani repudiated the avant-garde's claim to being completely new and its hegemony. Watkin found Van Doesburg's statements 'hollow and pretentious'.[49] In his study of German modern architecture, Lampugnani argued that the division between traditional and modern was less clear-cut than supposed, so that the whole notion of tradition and innovation was in need of revision. Rather than turning their backs on traditions altogether, the designers had been looking for a redefinition of tradition and principles. These writers also pointed out that new developments are not the exclusive preserve of architects and artists of the modern avant-garde, but part of much wider cultural tendencies.[50]

Thanks to a superb study stemming from just such a wide cultural approach, the Maison d'Artiste can now be viewed in a new light and the *Gesamtkunstwerk* has acquired yet another (additional) layer of meaning. In *De nieuwe mens*, the architectural historian Auke van der Woud gives a new perspective on the theme of awareness and experience by highlighting the 'panoptic gaze'. In that way of perceiving, an individual is totally absorbed in the moment, as for example when watching a film, but also quickly forgets that moment only to become absorbed in a new experience. The impression does not refer to something different or something higher, nor to norms and values, but is pure and genuine. Van Doesburg's Dada actions in 1923 were manifestations of that immediacy. With that panoptic gaze and ephemeral impression, mass culture had made its entry at the beginning of the twentieth century, according to Van der Woud, and he interprets this as a fundamental break with the preceding period. The new culture 'provided no direction, only freedom and an overwhelming number of possibilities'.[51]

61 Gerrit Rietveld and Truus Schröder, house for Mrs Schröder (the Rietveld-Schröder House), Utrecht, just after completion in c. 1924. Although the house was published in *De Stijl*, it was not until the second half of the twentieth century that it became a canonical work of De Stijl architecture.
Het Nieuwe Instituut, Rotterdam

**43** Hitchcock 1929, p. 361.
**44** Giedion 1941, p. 361.
**45** Giedion 1941, pp. 89–90; Giedion published the architectural analysis Van Doesburg had reproduced in his Bauhausbuch, Van Doesburg 1925a, fig. 3.
**46** Dettingmeijer 2010, p. 25.
**47** Hitchcock 1958, p. 377; Benevolo 1960 (1971), vol. II, pp. 409-410.
**48** Brown 1958, pp. 56–60; Bless 1982, p. 205 ff.; Troy 1983, pp. 116-121; Blotkamp 1984, pp. 11-13.
**49** Watkin 1986, p. 597.
**50** Lampugnani and Schneider 1992, p. 9.
**51** Van der Woud 2015, pp. 301–306, quotation p. 303.

62 Theo van Doesburg and Cornelis van Eesteren, counter-construction of Maison d'Artiste in colour by Theo van Doesburg, after 1923
Het Nieuwe Instituut, Rotterdam

63 Theo van Doesburg and Cornelis van Eesteren, Maison d'Artiste, colour sketch for the south elevation by Theo van Doesburg, with indications of glass panels, 1923
Het Nieuwe Instituut, Rotterdam

64 Theo van Doesburg and Cornelis van Eesteren, Maison d'Artiste model, 1923. View from above
Het Nieuwe Instituut, Rotterdam

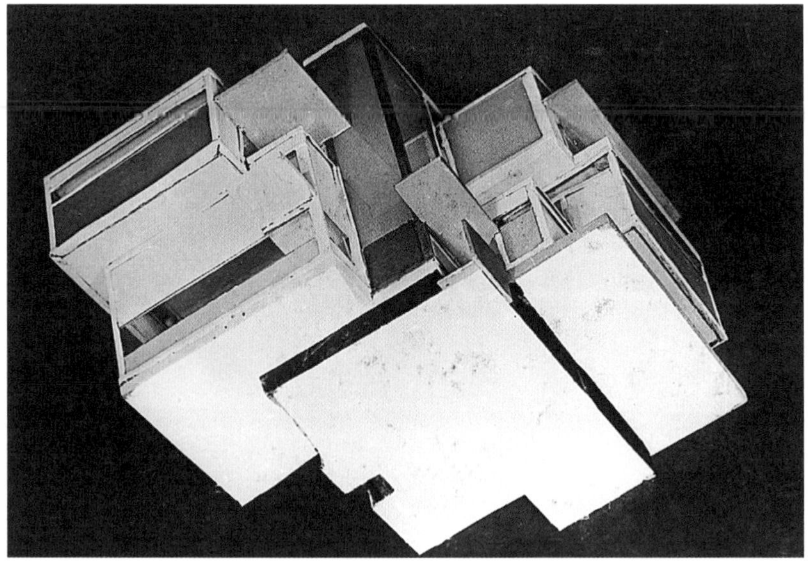

65 Theo van Doesburg and Cornelis van Eesteren, d'Artiste model, 1923. View from below
Het Nieuwe Instituut, Rotterdam

66 Theo van Doesburg and Cornelis van Eesteren, Maison d'Artiste model, 1923. Including view of music room on first floor
Het Nieuwe Instituut, Rotterdam

67 Theo van Doesburg and Cornelis van Eesteren, Maison d'Artiste model, 1923. Left on ground floor the double-height studio, staircase in centre, to right on first floor the music room
Het Nieuwe Instituut, Rotterdam

68 Theo van Doesburg and Cornelis van Eesteren,
Maison d'Artiste, 1923. Plan of ground floor
Het Nieuwe Instituut, Rotterdam

69 Theo van Doesburg and Cornelis van Eesteren,
Maison d'Artiste, 1923. Plan of first floor
Het Nieuwe Instituut, Rotterdam

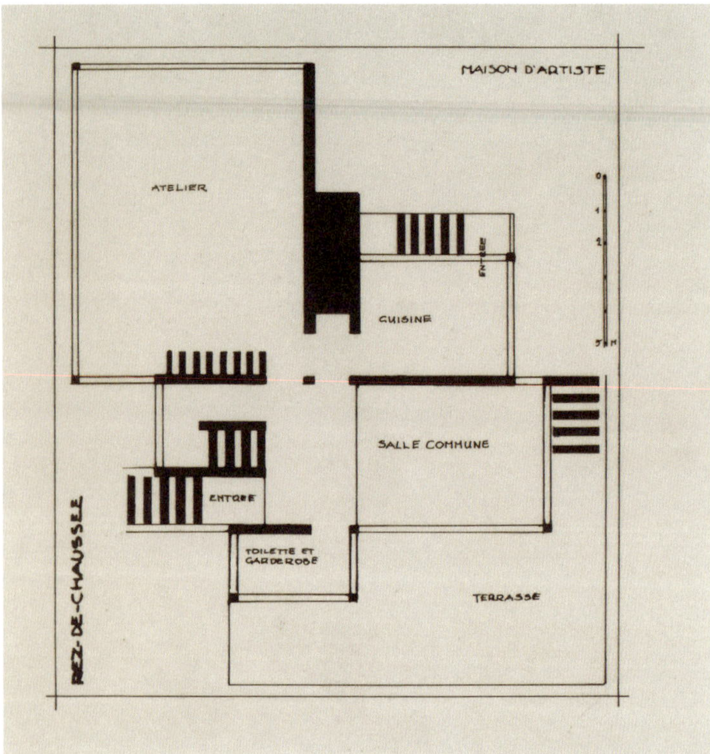


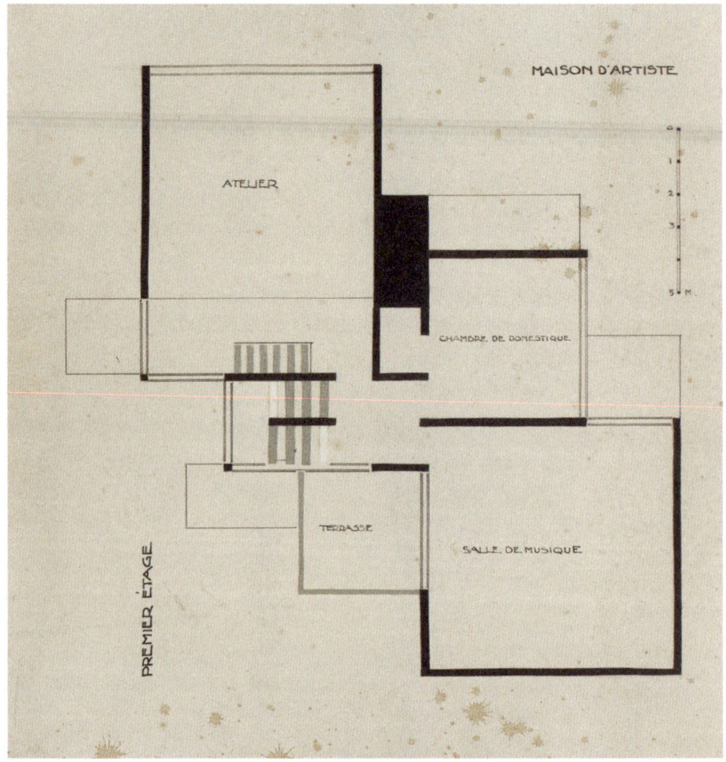

70 Theo van Doesburg and Cornelis van Eesteren, Maison d'Artiste, 1923. Plan of second floor
Het Nieuwe Instituut, Rotterdam

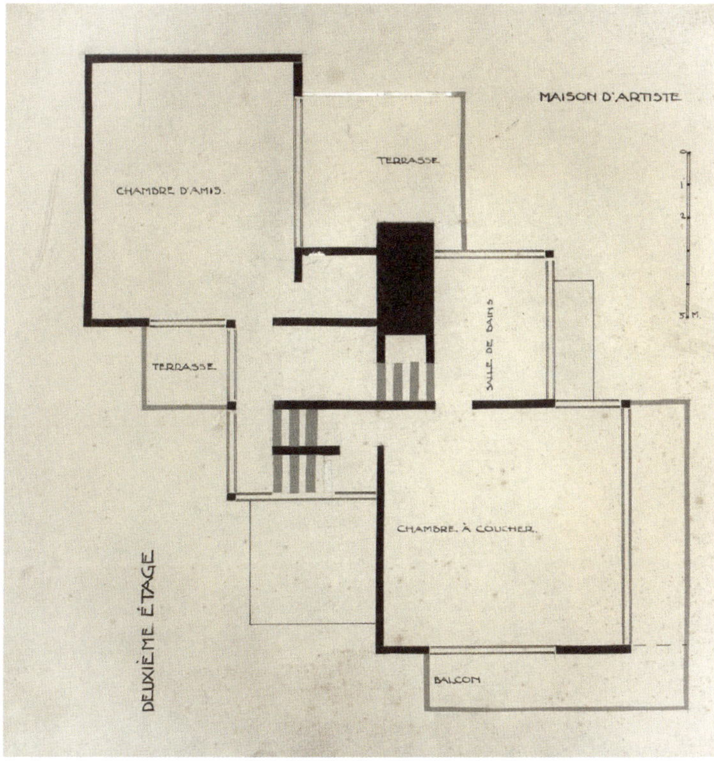


71 Theo van Doesburg and Cornelis van Eesteren, Maison d'Artiste, 1923. Plan of third floor
Het Nieuwe Instituut, Rotterdam

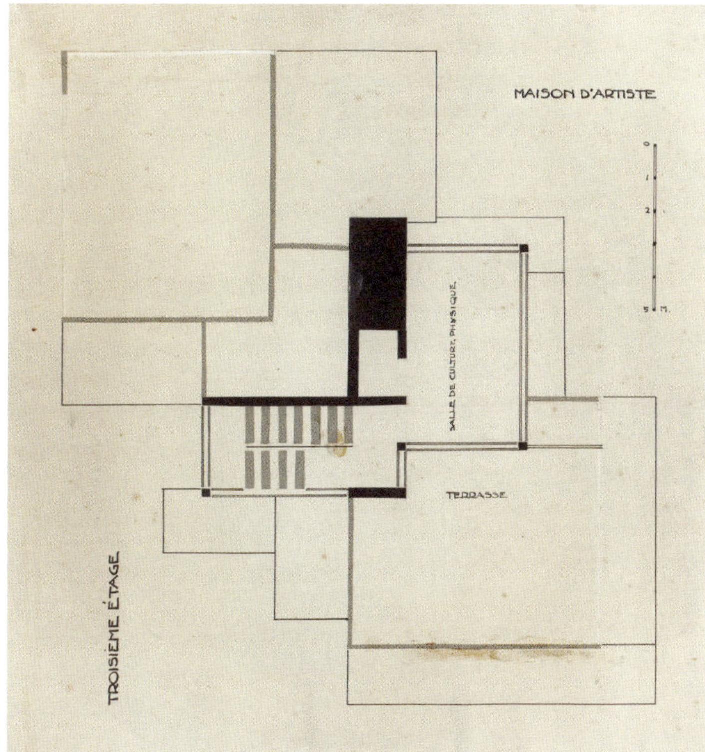

72 Theo van Doesburg and Cornelis van Eesteren, Maison d'Artiste, 1923. Design for the four elevations. As far as is known, the only surviving drawing of all four elevations
Het Nieuwe Instituut, Rotterdam

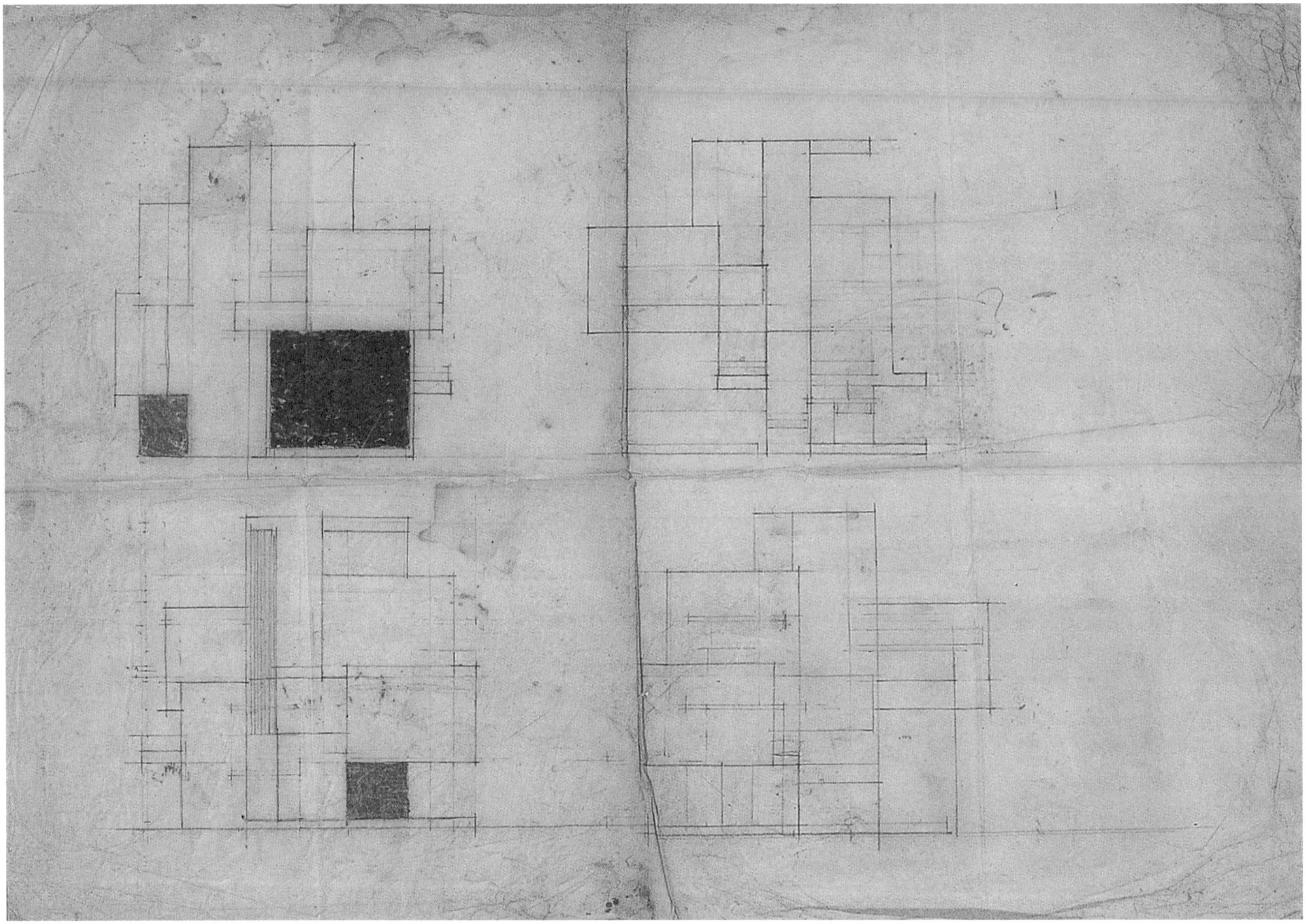

73 Theo van Doesburg and Cornelis van Eesteren,
Maison d'Artiste, c. 1923, axonometric
Het Nieuwe Instituut, Rotterdam

74 Theo van Doesburg and Cornelis van Eesteren,
Maison Particulière, 1923, axonometric
Het Nieuwe Instituut, Rotterdam

# Maison Particulière

75 Theo van Doesburg and Cornelis van Eesteren, Maison Particulière, 1923, plan of ground floor
Het Nieuwe Instituut, Rotterdam

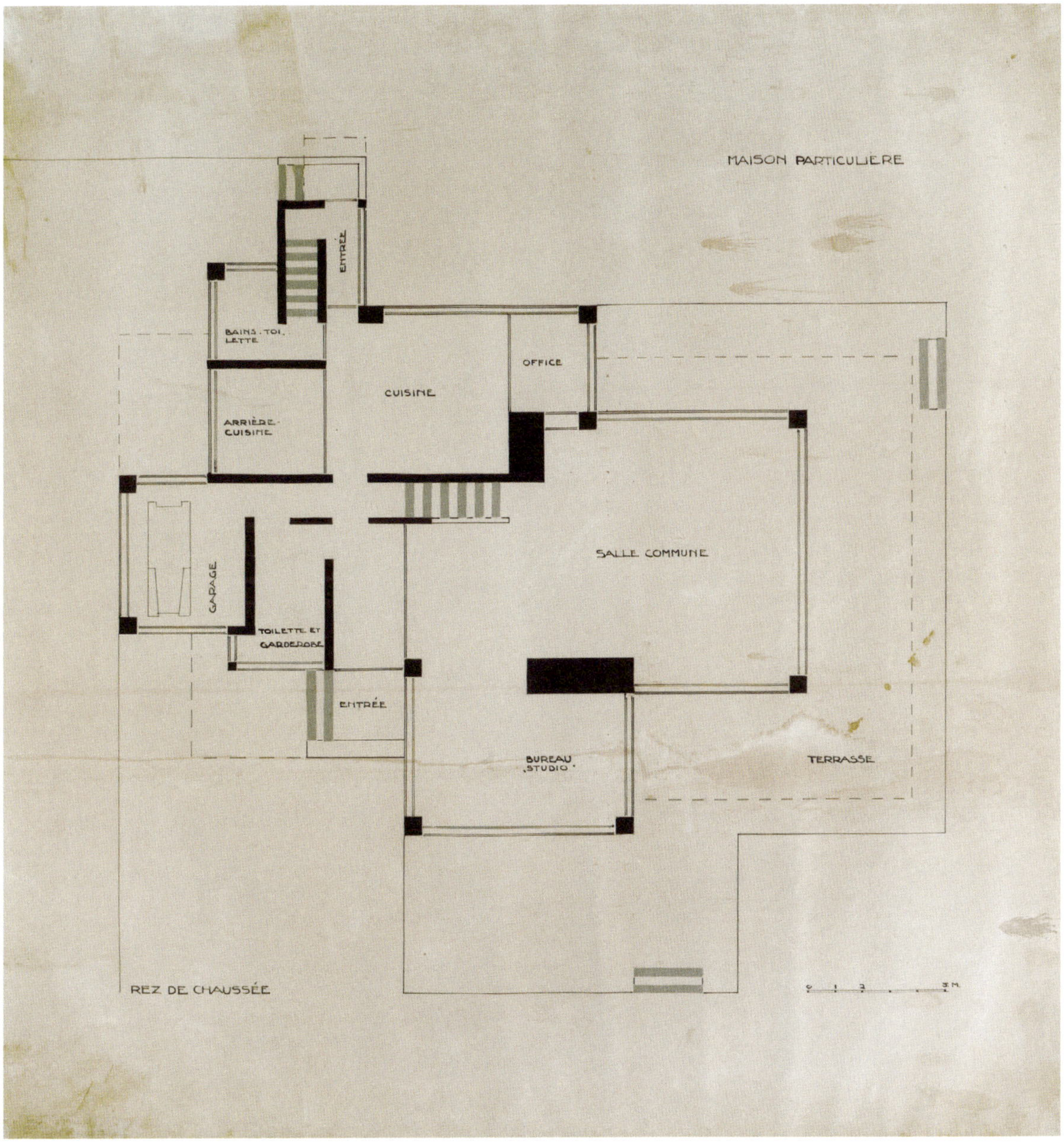

76 Theo van Doesburg and Cornelis van Eesteren,
Maison Particulière, 1923, plan of first floor
Het Nieuwe Instituut, Rotterdam

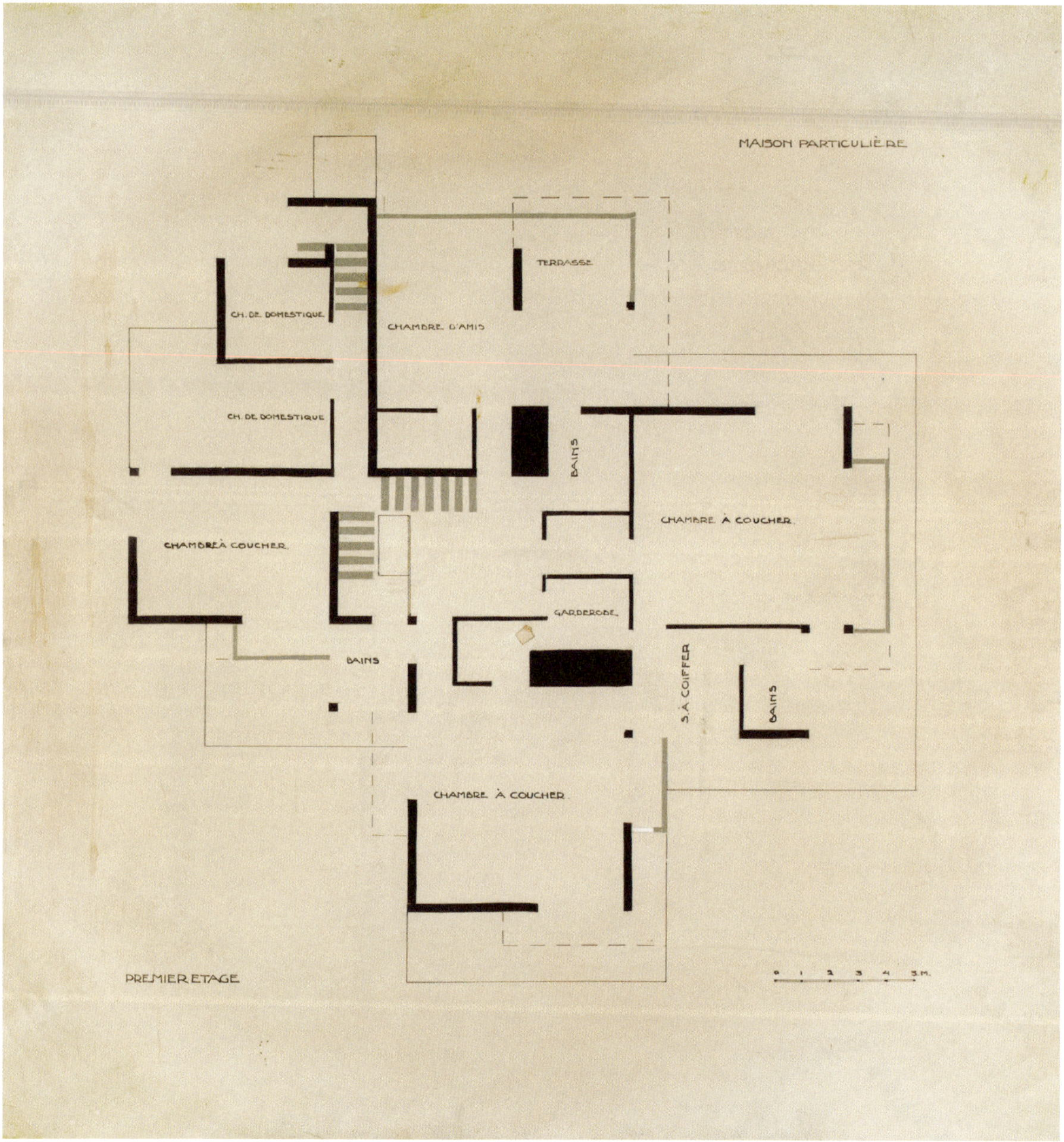

77 Theo van Doesburg and Cornelis van Eesteren, Maison Particulière, 1923, plan of second floor
Het Nieuwe Instituut, Rotterdam

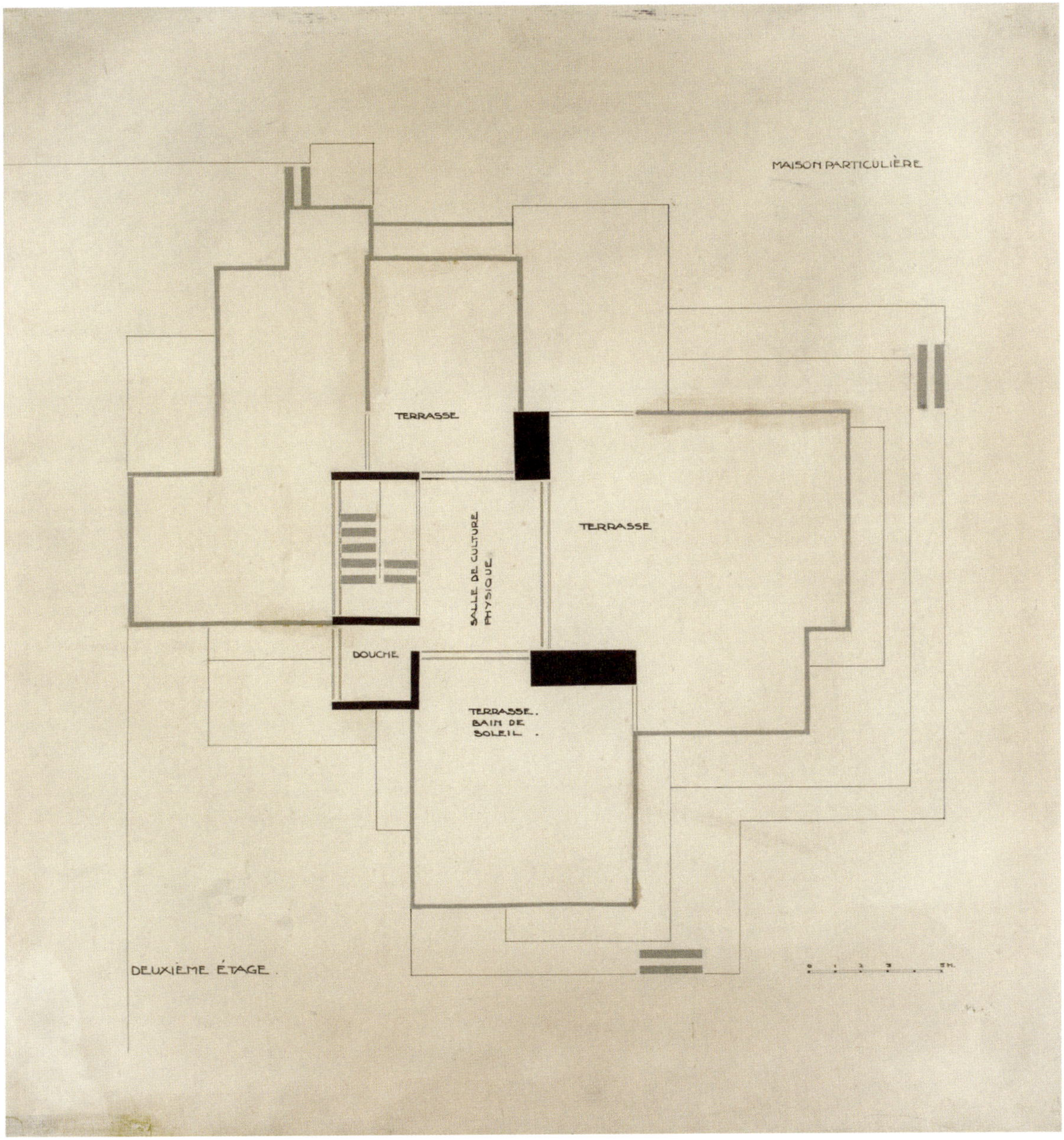

78 Theo van Doesburg and Cornelis van Eesteren,
Maison Particulière, 1923, north elevation
Het Nieuwe Instituut, Rotterdam

79 Theo van Doesburg and Cornelis van Eesteren,
Maison Particulière, 1923, east elevation
Het Nieuwe Instituut, Rotterdam

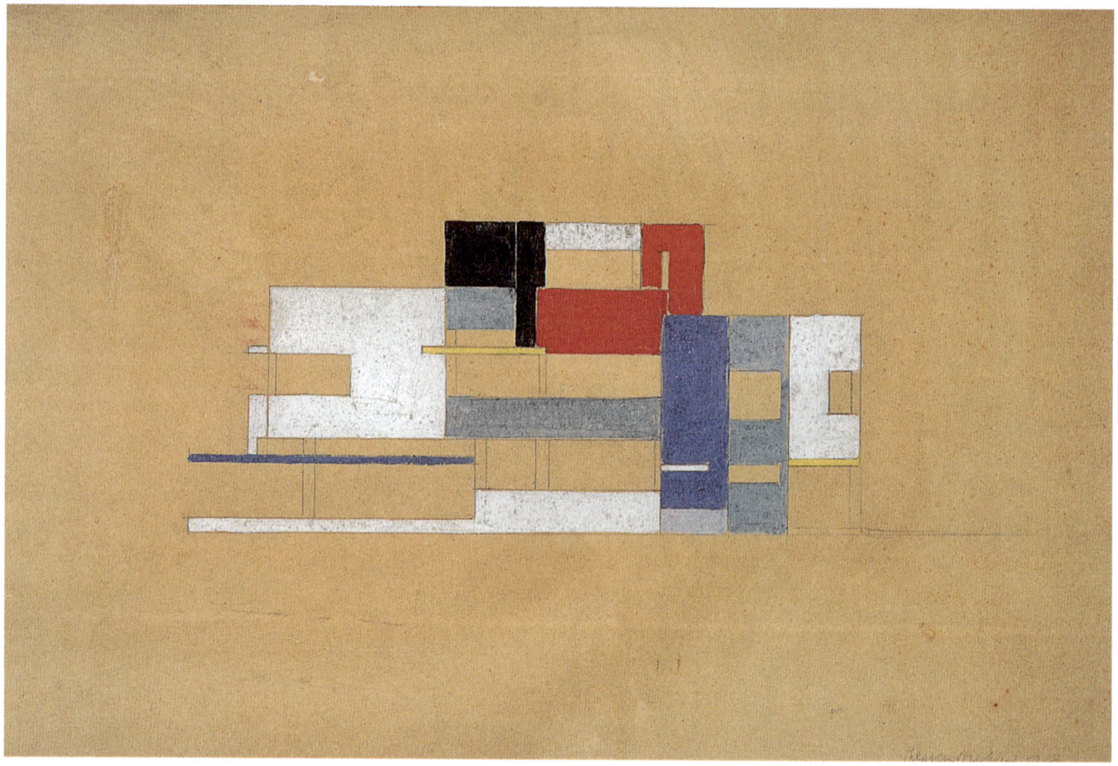

80 Theo van Doesburg and Cornelis van Eesteren, Maison Particulière, 1923, south elevation
Het Nieuwe Instituut, Rotterdam

81 Theo van Doesburg and Cornelis van Eesteren, Maison Particulière, 1923, west elevation
Het Nieuwe Instituut, Rotterdam

82 Theo van Doesburg and Cornelis van Eesteren, maquette Maison Particulière, 1923, photo
Het Nieuwe Instituut, Rotterdam

83 Theo van Doesburg, counter-construction in circle, c. 1923
Museum of Modern Art, New York, the Joan and Lester Avnet Collection

84 Theo van Doesburg and Cornelis van Eesteren, Maison Rosenberg (Hôtel Particulier), model produced by G.T. Rietveld in 1951 for the De Stijl exhibition in the Stedelijk Museum Amsterdam.
Het Nieuwe Instituut, Rotterdam

# Maison Rosenberg (Hôtel Particulier)

85 Theo van Doesburg and Cornelis van Eesteren,
Maison Rosenberg (Hôtel Particulier), 1923,
plan of ground floor
Het Nieuwe Instituut, Rotterdam

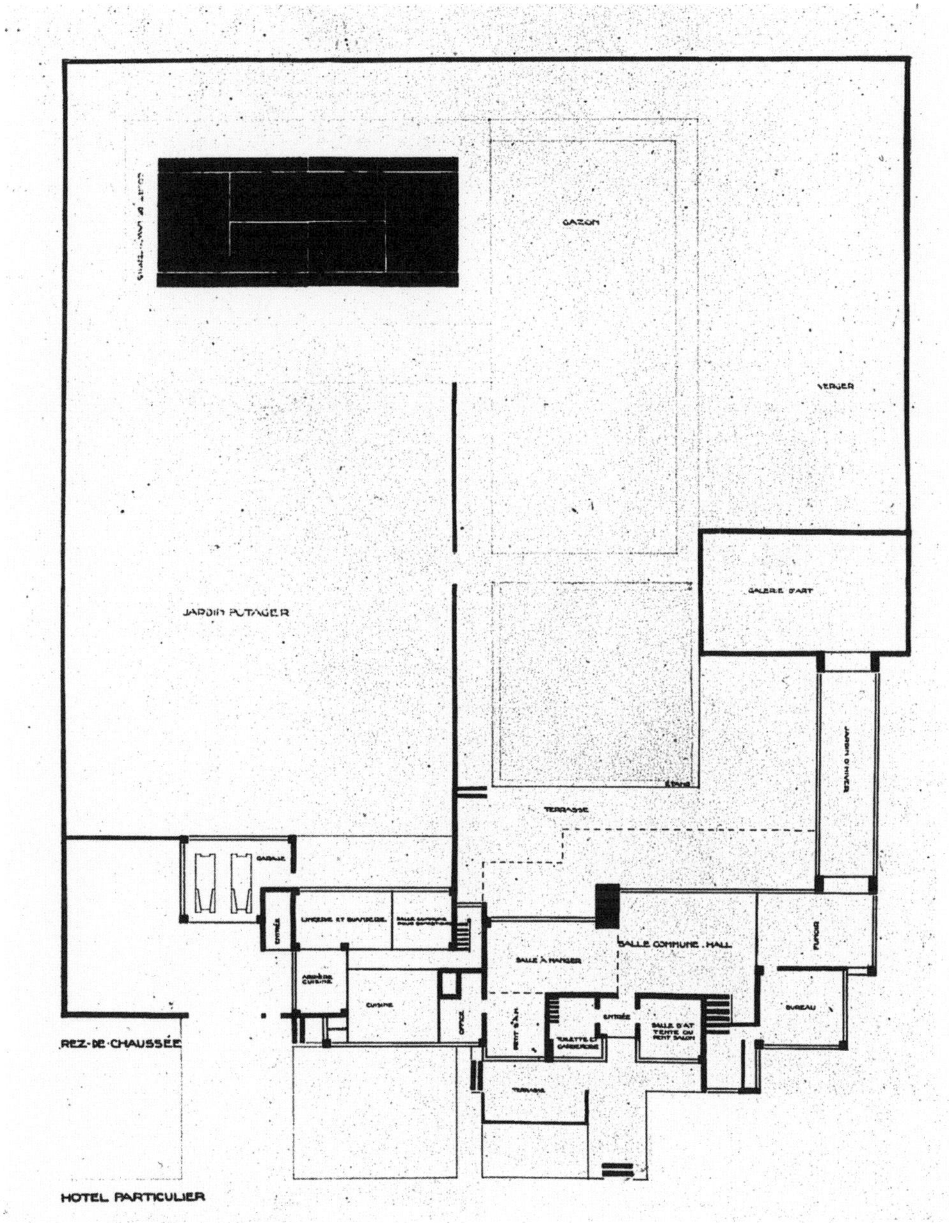

86 Theo van Doesburg and Cornelis van Eesteren,
Maison Rosenberg (Hôtel Particulier), 1923,
plan of first floor
Het Nieuwe Instituut, Rotterdam

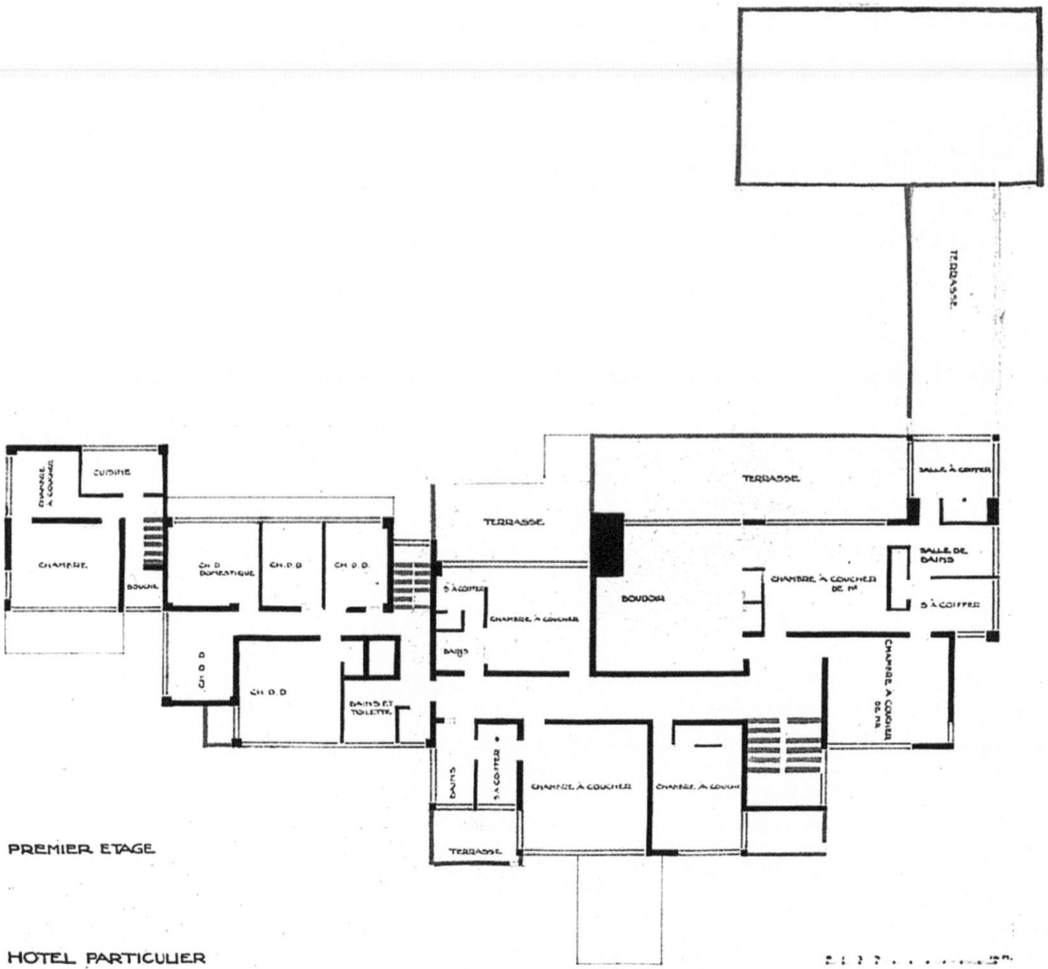

87 Theo van Doesburg and Cornelis van Eesteren,
Maison Rosenberg (Hôtel Particulier), 1923,
plan of second floor
Het Nieuwe Instituut, Rotterdam

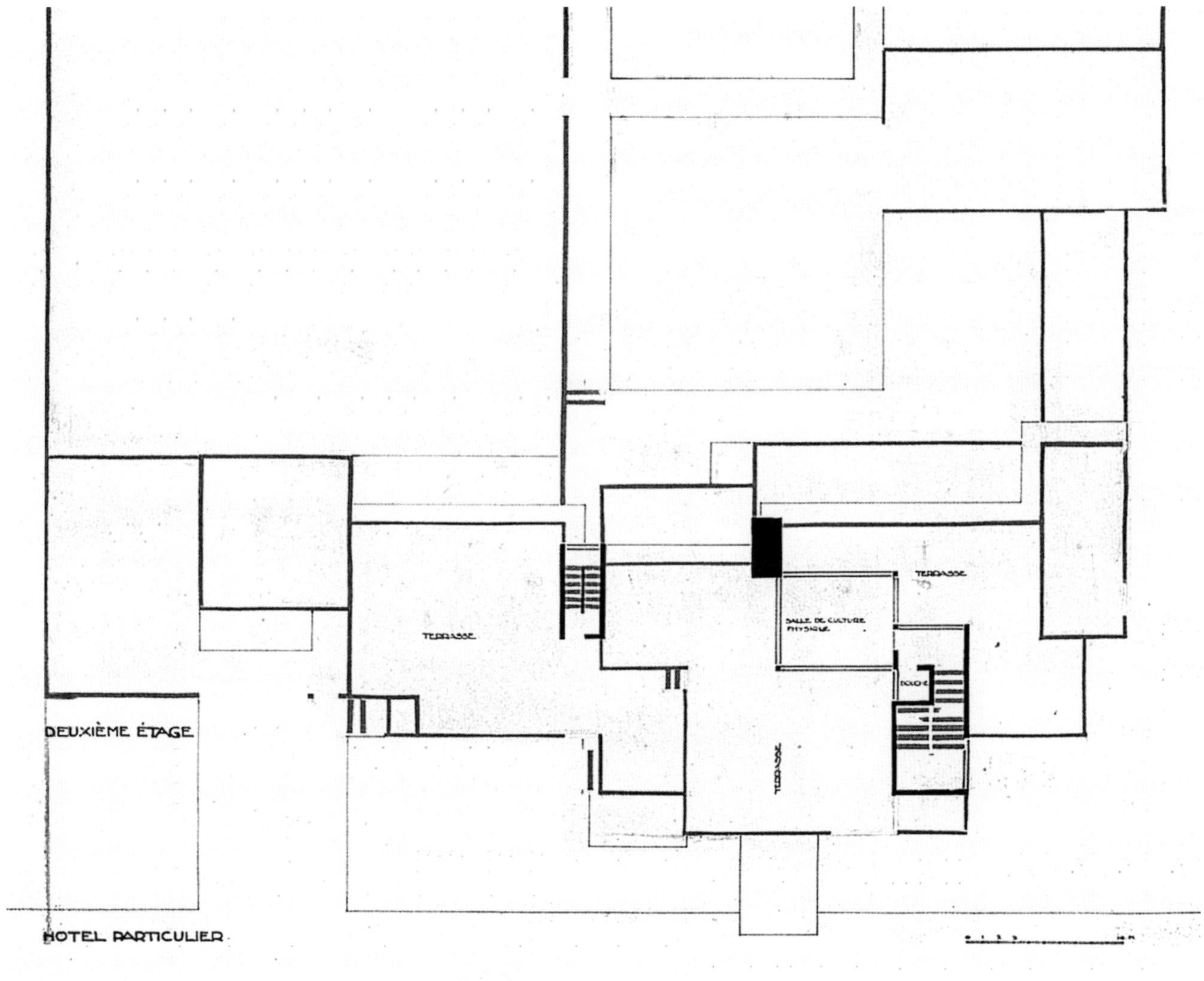

88–91 Theo van Doesburg and Cornelis van Eesteren, Maison Rosenberg (Hôtel Particulier), 1923, top left: southeast elevation, bottom left: northwest elevation, top right: northeast elevation, bottom right: southwest elevation. Het Nieuwe Instituut, Rotterdam

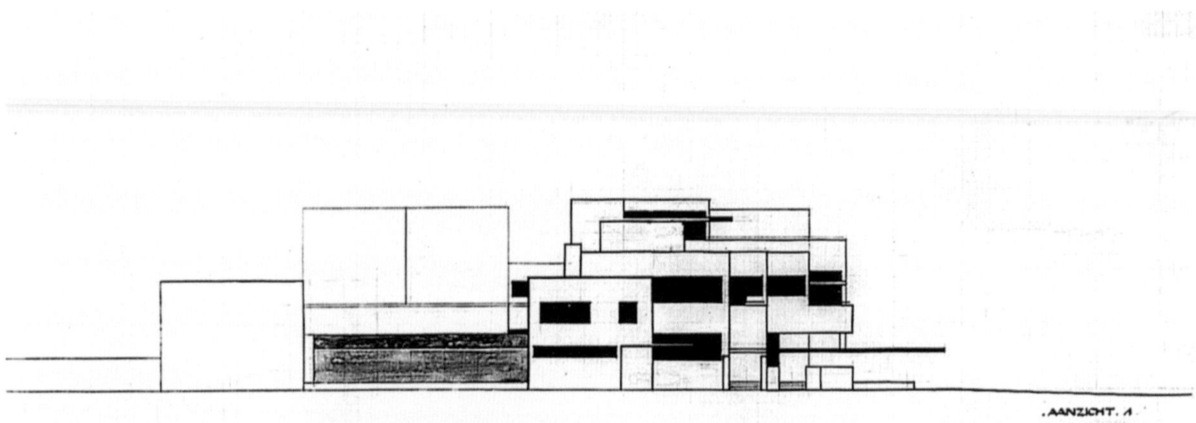


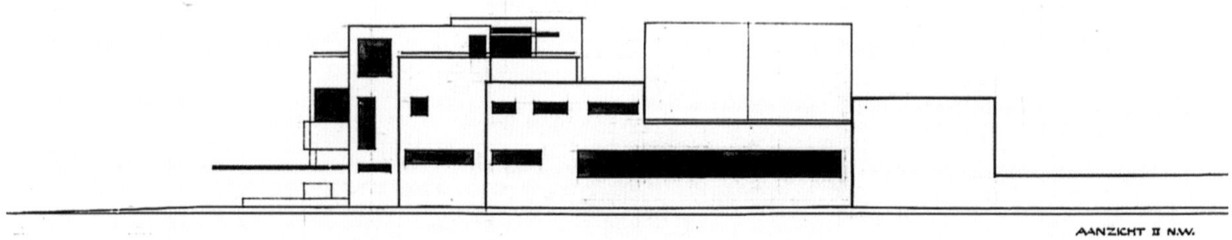

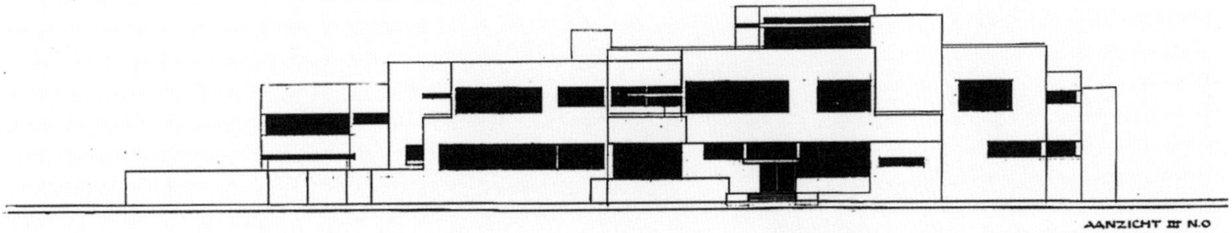
AANZICHT III N.O

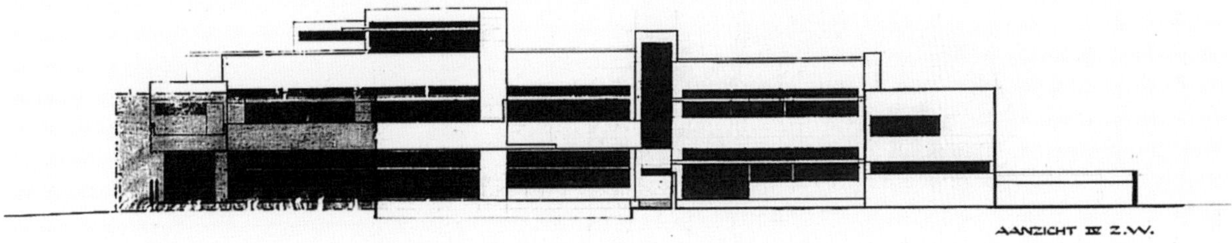
AANZICHT IV Z.W.

92 Maison d'Artiste located in Museumpark Rotterdam, c. 2006. Presentation model (1:500) of a location study of an unrealized design by V. Veldhuijzen van Zanten
Stichting Realisatie Maison d'Artiste / Photo Luuk de Boer

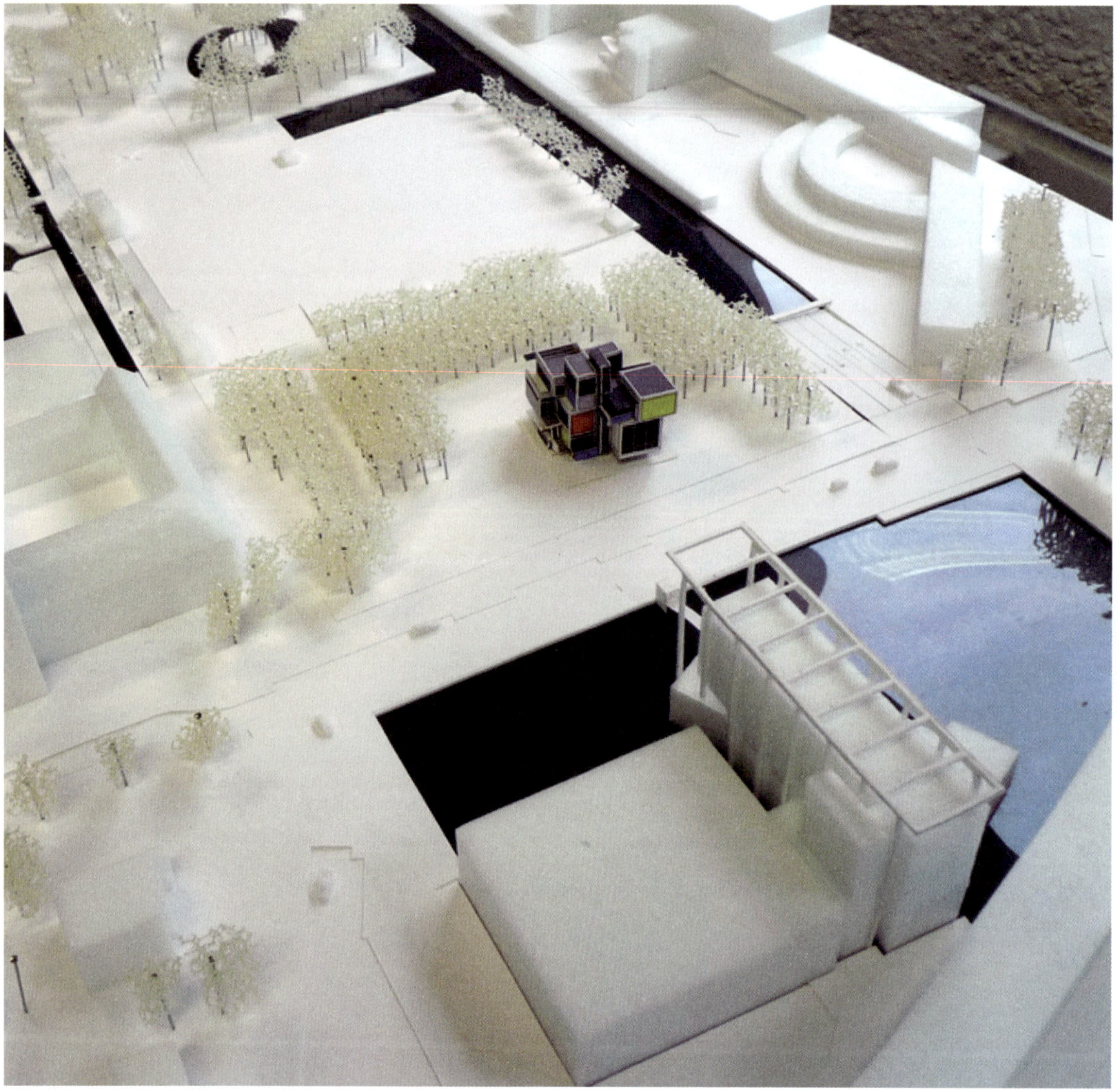

Dolf Broekhuizen

# Client wanted
# Possibilities and dilemmas surrounding realization

## Finishing the score

One of the essential ideas underpinning the Maison d'Artiste is the synthesis of painting, architecture and life in a *Gesamtkunstwerk*. A three-dimensional, full-scale realization would allow the Maison d'Artiste to be part of the lives of visitors and users. But what exactly would someone experience in such a late realization? The 1923 design for the Maison d'Artiste is unfinished. Were it to be built, therefore, it would always be regarded as a historical design that was elaborated at a later date. It could perhaps be compared with an unfinished score that is finished posthumously by a different composer, or a novel that has been translated. In any realization designers would have to make decisions about the detailing with respect to construction, material and colour. Moreover, it might prove necessary to integrate a different function into the design, possibly requiring modifications and at the very least an interior design concept. Finally, there are nowadays new requirements regarding fire safety, accessibility and energy management. This chapter explores the possibilities and the dilemmas surrounding the realization of the Maison d'Artiste.

## Wild schemes and detailed ideas

Over the years, various initiators have seriously considered the possibility of building the Maison d'Artiste, although many of the ideas never got beyond the stage of a cursory sketch, an exploratory talk or a wildly impractical scheme. Even one of the original designers gave it some thought. In the years 1983–1984, when there were several major exhibitions about De Stijl, Van Eesteren himself broached the idea of a full-scale realization of the Maison d'Artiste.[1] In the decades that followed, the idea of a 1:1 realization occasionally popped up on the agendas of cultural institutions and foundations. Of importance in all these initiatives were not only the basic questions of how, why and where, but also what function the new pavilion should have. An operational model that guarantees long-term use is a key condition for anyone contemplating subsidizing or financing the construction.

The Stichting Realisatie Maison d'Artiste (Foundation for the Realization of Maison d'Artiste, SRMA) has been pursuing the goal of construction since 2004.[2] The foundation's prime mover, architect Victor Veldhuijzen van Zanten, had already pointed out in the 1990s that a full-scale realization would serve to highlight the merits of Van Eesteren and Van Doesburg as architects. The foundation sees realization in the vicinity of Het Nieuwe Instituut (formerly the Netherlands Architecture Institute) in Rotterdam as a valuable addition to that institution's collection [figs. 92–96]. Moreover, programming a cultural and public function on the ground and first floors, and a semi-public function on the second floor, would serve to bolster the cultural infrastructure.[3] One of several potential users is the local architecture centre AIR in combination with an 'artist in residence'. But other locations and users have also been considered by the foundation, such as the post-war model village of Nagele in the Noordoost Polder, and in the vicinity of the Gemeentemuseum in The Hague, which strives to present a 'total picture' of De Stijl.[4]

1 Van Eesteren made this known in 1984 in a conversation with Tjaarda Mees and Victor Veldhuijzen van Zanten about the 1983 models, and a cardboard cut-out (1:100) made a year after the De Stijl exhibition in the Haags Gemeentemuseum. Interview with Victor Veldhuijzen van Zanten, Rotterdam, 23 November 2015.

2 The Stichting Realisatie Maison d'Artiste was founded on 23 November 2004 and registered with the Rotterdam Chamber of Commerce on 28 December 2004.

3 *Ontwerp realisatie Maison d'Artiste, 2006*, SRMA. Proposed team in 2006: architects, Victor Veldhuijzen van Zanten and Wessel de Jonge; construction, structural engineering and building services consultants, DHV Bouw en Industrie; supervisor, Hubert-Jan Henket. According to a 2006 estimate carried out by the foundation, construction would cost around two million euros (excl. VAT). Interview with Victor Veldhuijzen van Zanten, Rotterdam, 22 February 2016.

4 Interview with Victor Veldhuijzen van Zanten, Rotterdam, 22 February 2016; for Haags Gemeentemuseum see: Tempel, Janssen and Van der Tholen 2011; Janssen and White 2011.

Since 2013 the foundation has been optimistic that a mooted collaboration with the Dutch Drawing Centre (DDC) will increase the chances of realization. As Reyn van der Lugt, one of the initiators from the DDC, remarked in a recent interview: 'As a new, still unknown organization, the Dutch Drawing Centre's desire for identity, visibility, permanent availability and a location close to cultural institutions fits in well with the aims of the Stichting Realisatie Maison d'Artiste.' Equally important is the affinity between the design and the Drawing Centre's envisaged programme: 'We aim to take a wide-ranging approach to the medium of drawing and that includes showing architectural drawings. Following the example of the New York Drawing Center, exhibitions, lectures and a 'drawer in residence' will focus attention on the many and varied facets of drawing. This building is a good vehicle for that broad programme because it coincides with Van Doesburg and Van Eesteren's notion of

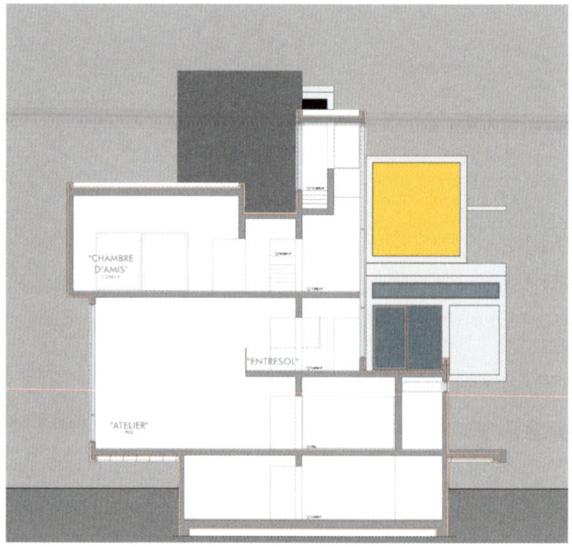


Design for Maison d'Artiste,
V. Veldhuijzen van Zanten, 2006
(unrealized)
Stichting Realisatie Maison d'Artiste

93 North elevation
94 One of the cross-sections

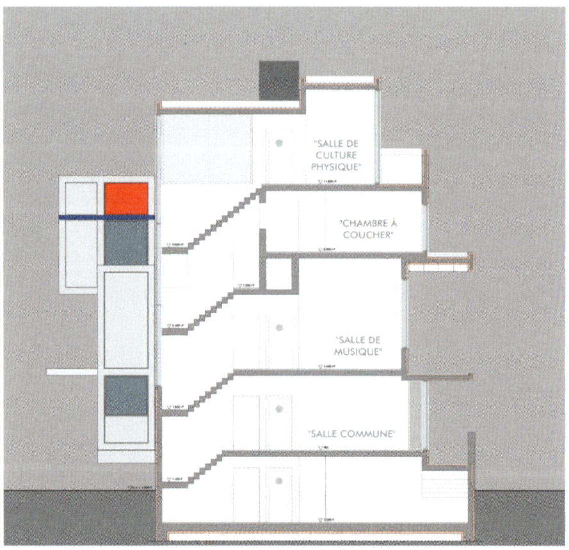


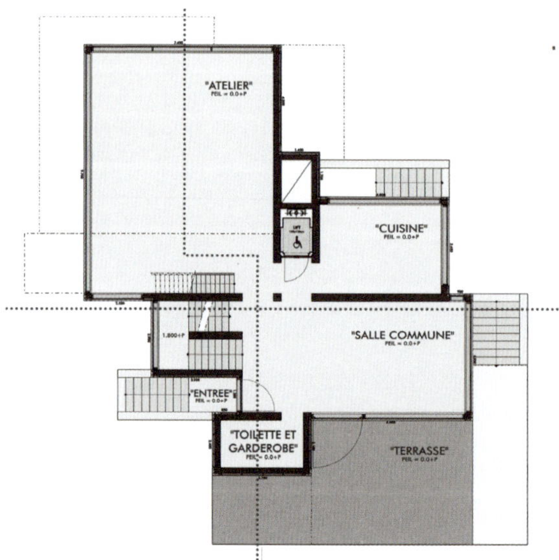


The rooms in Maison d'Artiste are distributed over several levels. There are no known 1923 cross-section drawings.
Stichting Realisatie Maison d'Artiste

95 Cross-section through staircase
96 Plan of ground floor. To increase accessibility, a lift was inserted into the design.

analysing art, architecture and design in terms of the drawing. Our programme respects that way of thinking, and that could also find expression in the way people experience the building. This would make it interesting for both the architecture enthusiast and the wider public.'[5] As yet, nothing has come of these plans.

In recent decades there have been other initiatives, too, although less detailed. In 1998, Maarten Kloos, former director of the Amsterdam architecture centre Arcam, considered building the Maison d'Artiste next to the temporarily empty pavilion by Renzo Piano on Oosterdok [fig. 97]. He tested the architectural design as new accommodation for Arcam, but this idea did not get any further than a free-thinking exercise. Maarten Kloos: 'I tried it out at the kitchen table, executing the design on a realistic scale. I made a few sketches to see whether it was possible to arrive at a usable building.'[6]

97 M. Kloos, photomontage of Maison d'Artiste on Oosterdok in Amsterdam, as premises for Arcam, the local architecture centre, 1998 (unrealized)
Private collection

In the context of the Amsterdam expansion areas designed by Van Eesteren (his 'magnum opus'), the pavilion would not only have served to highlight a prominent designer who was active in Amsterdam, and honour him posthumously, but the striking building would also have enhanced the organization's visibility in the city.[7]

5 Interview with Reyn van der Lugt, secretary of Stichting Dutch Drawing Centre, Rotterdam, 22 February 2016.

6 Interview with Maarten Kloos, former director of Arcam, 15 February 2016.

7 In 2003 a new design by René van Zuuk was realized on the foundations of the Renzo Piano pavilion. Groenendijk 2003.

The architect Mick Eekhout, who assessed the 'buildability' of the Maison d'Artiste in 2000 at the request of the Van Eesteren-Fluck & Van Lohuizen Stichting (EFL Stichting) [fig. 98], has suggested that if it were to be executed as a more or less demountable design, the pavilion could travel to international exhibitions. He devised a construction system that would make it possible to achieve the deep cantilevers [fig. 99].[8] As for motivation, he concluded: 'If the model were to be built on a true scale, the new building could stand as a manifestation of the enormous theoretical stimulus De Stijl gave to international architecture.'[9]

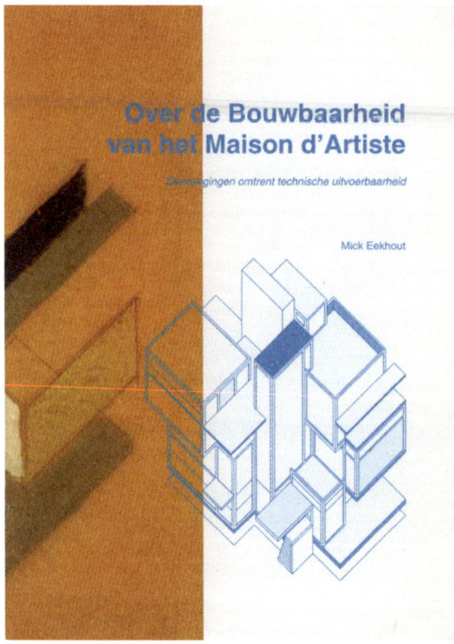


98 Cover of the publication by Mick Eekhout, '*Over de bouwbaarheid van het Maison d'Artiste*', 2000

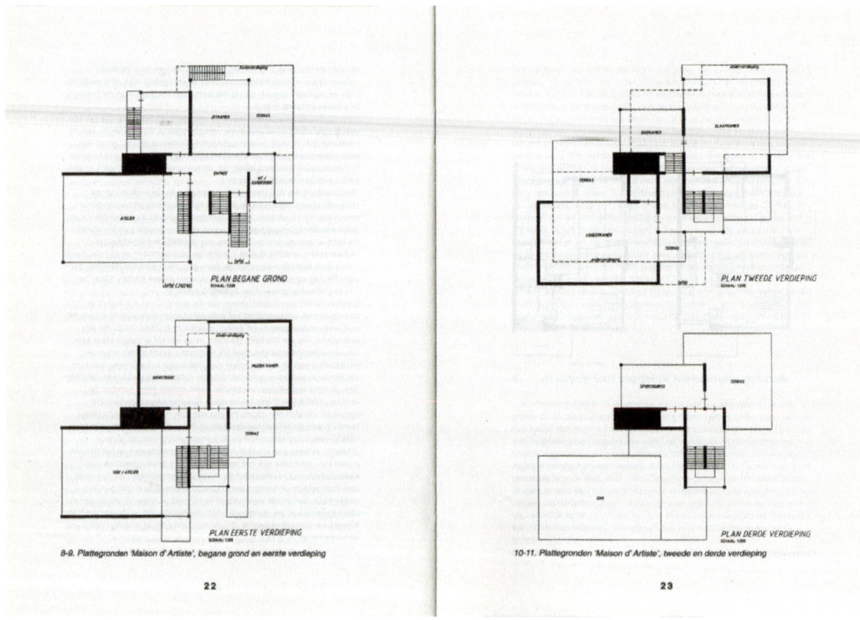


99 Mick Eekhout, analysis for realization of a constructional system for Maison d'Artiste, four floor plans, 2000 (unrealized). Indication of 'upper supporting structure' (cross-hatched) and 'lower supporting structure' (black). As Illustrated in Eekhout, *Over de Bouwbaarheid van het Maison d'Artiste*, 2000

## Basic questions

Before considering questions regarding the aim and potential functions of these attempts at realization, the fundamental questions about the possibility and desirability of realization need to be addressed. Critics argue that the image of the design would be distorted by late realization and that this might have the effect of eclipsing the authentic object. Proponents acknowledge that construction would be an interpretation (a translation) of the design, but maintain that it would render the manifesto character of the original 1923 design visible in a different way and enrich our understanding of it.[10] In 2008 a group of international experts came to a positive conclusion on the question of whether construction would strengthen the design as manifesto. This committee, consisting of museum directors and experts in the field of architecture, argued that 'the "Maison d'Artiste" should be viewed as an untapped gold mine that merited further exploration in the form of analyses and interpretations. The realization of a full-scale interpretation could fundamentally contribute to our understanding and our awareness regarding this intellectual legacy and thus also enrich the understanding of our own background and history.'[11] With this statement the committee added its weight to the idea that construction is a worthwhile means of increasing understanding and the experiential value, although the members acknowledged that counter-arguments were possible. In the case of the Maison d'Artiste, while 'doing nothing' preserves the existing image, it forfeits the opportunity to experience a full-scale rendering of the design.[12]

This leads to another basic question: what is the authentic design? There are different ways of looking at this. The idea of authenticity acquires a special meaning in the case of late realization.[13] Because a full-scale Maison d'Artiste has never existed, a full-scale realization cannot be a reconstruction or a restoration, unlike, for example, the envisaged reconstruction of the Philips Pavilion (1958), where the initiators are able to consult a previous realization of the design.[14] The new-build design for the Maison d'Artiste will contain references to the past, but which particular ones is not pre-determined. Is the authentic object primarily the (design) idea, the concept that underpins a project, or do material and physical aspects weigh more heavily? If the aim is to realize the materials, construction method and finishes of the historical design, as well as the historical forms and spaces, the resulting image will be one that has never existed. According to Wessel de Jonge, Professor of Heritage and Design at TU Delft, and involved in the initiatives to rebuild the Philips Pavilion, that impression should not be created in the case of the Maison d'Artiste.[15] De Jong: 'I think it's a good principle to avoid giving the impression that the building was actually built in the 1920s. Theoretically it might have been possible. I can imagine that people might look at the construction techniques and materials that the two men employed in other projects at that time, and derive the materialization of the new design from that. But you'd be misleading people completely by suggesting with a retro design that the studio house had once actually existed.' That does not mean, De Jonge adds, that a designer is completely free to give their own interpretation of the unelaborated design: 'I'm in favour of further research into the original design: how did Van Doesburg and Van Eesteren themselves approach the materialization of the Maison d'Artiste, for example? For a designer such an overview is necessary in order to be able to make appropriate design decisions, rather than going right off the rails with an unfounded contemporary interpretation in, say, polyester, as was once proposed.'[16]

## An unfinished design: construction, materialization, colour

Those who have researched the possibilities for realizing the Maison d'Artiste point to the unfinished and experimental nature of the design, which had come about in an exchange of ideas between the painter Theo van Doesburg and the younger architect Cornelis van Eesteren. Some argue that the Maison d'Artiste and the Maison Particulière were created as 'purely experimental investigations which did not take financial or technical considerations into account.'[17]

Designers and art historians who have meticulously reconstructed the working method based on an analysis of the design and archival material, explain discrepancies between the drawings and the model in the photographs as mainly the result of the exploratory nature of the design process. It is a risky business making precise statements about what came earlier or later, and what can be regarded as a preliminary or a more definitive phase. The relatively short time span during which the painter and architect laboured to get the models ready in time for the opening, explains differences between drawings and models. It is not even known whether the floor plans were finished earlier than the models, which they worked on up to the very last moment because of the colour design. The model has the character of a design maquette rather than a genuine

**8** For an (unbuilt) full-scale realization he suggested 'steel edge profiles … filled with steel sandwich floors' and a system of 'perpendicularly intersecting trimmer joists, with columns above and below' for all floors. Eekhout 2000, p. 30.

**9** Eekhout 2000, p. 34.

**10** Museums in particular recognize the experiential value of reconstructions and objects that a visitor can 'enter'. Recently a new dimension was added to this by the Art Institute of Chicago. In 2016, in the context of an exhibition of the Vincent van Gogh painting *De slaapkamer* (The Bedroom, 1888–1889), a life-size version of the bedroom in the painting was built, which can be booked via Airbnb.

**11** Members of the international 'Maison d'Artiste realization review committee': Pi de Bruijn, Manfred Bock, Marc Dubois, Sjarel Ex, Arthur Rüegg, Evert van Straaten; unavoidably absent: Ole Bouman, Francis Strauven. Review committee's conclusion and recommendations, 21 March 2008, SRMA.

**12** Formally speaking, permission for realization is a responsibility of the designers and/or their legal representatives: Van Doesburg's heir is Wies van Moorsel, Van Eesteren's is the Van Eesteren–Fluck & Van Lohuizen Stichting.

**13** For the broader discussion about authenticity and reconstruction, see the chapter by Paul Meurs in this book.

**14** Wessel de Jonge carried out a feasibility study for the reconstruction of the Philips Pavilion: De Jonge 2007; see also Wever 2015, pp. 148-149.

**15** In architectural circles a distinction is made between 'design authenticity' and 'material authenticity'. Interview with Wessel de Jonge, Delft, 15 February 2016.

**16** Interview with Wessel de Jonge, Delft, 15 February 2016.

**17** Boekraad 1983b, p. 75.

presentation maquette. It is a sketch design, the technical, structural and material aspects of which have not (yet) been worked out in detail.[18]

Many of the key questions in the context of a full-scale realization, those relating to the construction and choice of materials, remained undecided in the 1923 design. There are some indications for the materialization, but they are incomplete or unclear. According to an annotation (in German) along the edge of one of the model photographs, the designers had the following materials in mind: 'Eisen, Spiegelglas, Beton, Farbe, Email, Alluminium, uns.' (iron, plate glass, concrete, colour, enamel, aluminium, etc.), but whoever penned the note (Van Doesburg or Van Eesteren) did not specify where the materials should be used [fig. 100]. Elevations and floor plans are equally unhelpful owing to the scale and the way they were drawn, and to the lack of a legend. Two designers who have researched the supporting structure, Mick Eekhout (2000) and Victor Veldhuijzen van Zanten (2006), assume that the 1923 design was designed with a reinforced concrete structure as the main supporting structure.[19] Eekhout, former professor of product development at TU Delft, finds a connection with the Dom-Ino principle that Le Corbusier had published in 1915.[20] Historians Evert van Straaten (1988) and Manfred Bock (2001) on the other hand suspect that a composite frame or a steel skeleton is meant, with infill elements in reinforced concrete.[21] During new archival research undertaken for this book, evidence for a steel skeleton as supporting structure came to light. A handwritten explanation on a list of works for the exhibition in Galerie L'Effort Moderne, gives the chief materials for the execution of the building as iron and glass: 'construction en fer et en verre'.[22]
In combination with the note on the model photo, where 'Eisen' is the first word mentioned, this gives the impression that iron

100 Theo van Doesburg and Cornelis van Eesteren, retouched photo of Maison d'Artiste model, c. 1924. Around the edge, a note in German about the materials: 'Eisen, Spiegelglas, Beton, Farbe, Email, Alluminium, uns.', and title 'Exzentrische Konstruction eine Künstlerhaus' [sic] RKD – Netherlands Institute for Art History, The Hague

(or steel) was intended as the main supporting structure and concrete only for the infill elements. Construction using a steel skeleton also fits in with the more radical character of the cantilevered volumes of the Maison d'Artiste compared with the other two Paris models, which have more load-bearing walls. Making allowance for translation errors, reinforced concrete and glass ('construction en ciment armee et en glace') are named as the materials for the Maison Rosenberg, and concrete and glass

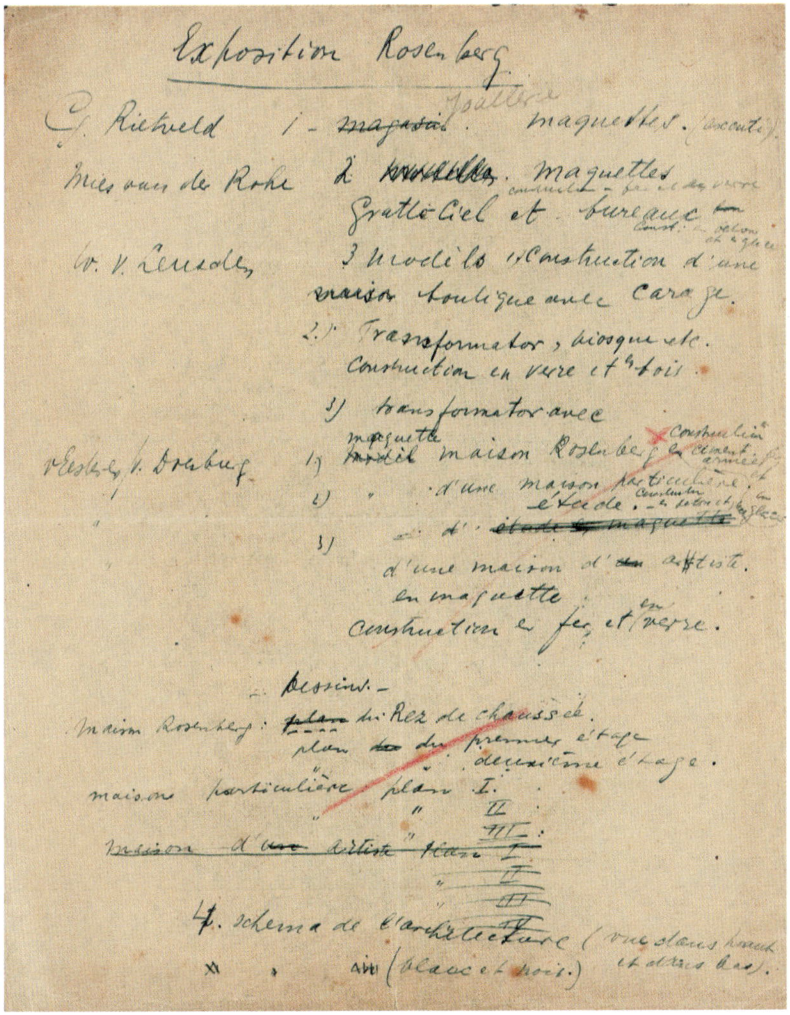
Exposition Rosenberg
G. Rietveld 1 - Joaillerie maquettes. (exécutée)
Mies van de Rohe 2. maquettes
Gratte-Ciel et bureaux
W. v. Leusden, 3 modèles construction d'une maison boutique avec Garage.
2. Transformator, kiosque etc. Construction en verre et bois.
3) transformator avec maquette
v. Eesteren v. Doesburg 1) maquette maison Rosenberg
2) d'une maison particulière
3) d'une maquette d'une maison d'artiste.
en maquette
construction en fer et verre.
Dessins. -
maison Rosenberg: du Rez de chaussée.
plan du premier étage
deuxième étage.
maison particulière plan I. II III
maison d'artiste plan I II III
4. schéma de l'architecture (blanc et noir.)

101 List of works exhibited in Galerie L'Effort Moderne, 1923. The material proposed for Maison d'Artiste – iron and glass – is mentioned halfway down the first right-hand page. RKD – Netherlands Institute for Art History, The Hague

('construction en beton et glace') for the Maison Particulière.[23] Because of the terseness, this text is open to several interpretations and is an indication of the desirability of further research.

## Colour research and materialization

Clues to the application of colours, such as materialization and position, are equally unclear. In the note around the edge of the aforementioned photograph, for example, 'Farbe' and 'Email' are listed separately, which makes it difficult to know whether 'Email' refers to the white and grey or red, blue and yellow coloured enamel facade cladding, which remain colourfast for longer than, say, painted wood. It is possible that enamel refers to the white glass that, according to a note on a design drawing, Van Doesburg wanted to use for the glazing of the staircase and which can be produced as enamelled white glass.[24] For his part, Van Eesteren attached great importance to the appearance: 'Many modern materials are so denaturalized that they contain all the colour possibilities. We have tried to achieve simultaneous colour unity,' he wrote in an elucidation of the Maison Particulière and the Maison d'Artiste published in 1931.[25] Reconstructions carried out by Tjaarda Mees, Frans Postma, Mick Eekhout and Victor Veldhuijzen van Zanten offer no unequivocal answers regarding the colour design for the Maison d'Artiste. If the maquette is taken as the starting point for the colour design, there are some black-and-white photographs of it in existence.[27] But the reconstruction of colours based on

**18** For the most detailed analyses of the authorship and intrinsic significance of the Maison d'Artiste see: Bock 2001.

**19** Eekhout 2000, pp. 27-28; V. Veldhuijzen van Zanten, *Ontwerp realisatie Maison d'Artiste, 2006*, SRMA.

**20** Eekhout 2000, pp. 27-28. Formulated at the behest of the EFL Stichting, which manages the estates of Cornelis van Eesteren and planner-urban designer T.K. van Lohuizen.

**21** 'Van Doesburg conceived the realization as a steel structure with reinforced concrete.' Van Straaten 1988, p. 142; 'The idea was probably rigid, coupled-together frames in which the walls and the window and door frames would be mounted.' Bock 2001, p. 192.

**22** This document has never previously been linked to the construction method. Handwritten list of exhibited works in 'Exposition Rosenberg', RKD VDA 1006.

**23** Handwritten list of exhibited works in 'Exposition Rosenberg', RKD VDA 1006; for a different version with translation suggestions see: HNI EEST 3.360; for translations during his Paris period, Van Eesteren consulted his landlady, whom he referred to as 'aunt' in his letters. Bock 2001, p. 120.

**24** With the aid of 'tin oxide and bone ash' colourless glass can be given a white enamel finish. For glass enamelling see: Sirag 1941, p. 367; the colour design for the facade is pictured in Van Straaten 1988, p. 142.

**25** Van Eesteren 1931, p. 38.

**26** Eekhout 2015, p. 15.

**27** Van Eesteren worked on the colour reconstruction of the Maison d'Artiste in 1968: HNI EEST 3.213-3.222.

an analysis of black-and-white photographs is notoriously complicated.[28] Other surviving information regarding the colours is terse and incomplete: there is one (sketchy) coloured counter-construction of the Maison d'Artiste and two unfinished facade drawings (with experimental daubs of colour).[29]

Apart from the obscurities, the lack of details presents another challenge for the buildability. Because there are no cross-sections, a full reconstruction of the internal organization is impossible. Especially with regard to the differences in level that are such a characteristic feature of the design, this can be seen as a great loss. In addition, many of the material details are unclear. Care is required in applying the analysis of reference projects like the studio home Van Doesburg had built to his own design in Meudon in 1929–1930 [figs. 102, 103]. The feasibility of certain aspects, such as the structure and the large glazed areas, is linked to the function to be housed in the building. Other aspects are theoretically feasible, but would probably need to be modified. Regulations relating to fire safety and accessibility might require a few adjustments to the original design, such as widening of the narrow stairs and the addition of a lift, which are mandatory for a public function.

102, 103 Theo van Doesburg, in collaboration with A. Elzas, House in Meudon (France), photo taken just after completion in 1930.
In 1929-1930 Van Doesburg designed a studio-house in which he lived for a few months
Left: street elevation, right: elevation with studio windows.
Het Nieuwe Instituut, Rotterdam

## The Maison d'Artiste as a source of inspiration

Based on the preceding analysis, one can conclude that the design is buildable, but that there is no agreement as to the best or most acceptable form of realization. The options are closely tied to where the emphasis is laid in appreciation for the design and to new circumstances (client, function, location). Were realization to go ahead, further historical research would need to be carried out, which might result in new proposals, including for the design. In principle, designers appear to be agreed that in addition to historical references, they should be free to use new, contemporary materials. The very fact that the design has never been built would seem to justify a new design, so long as the original design is treated with respect.

Apart from the execution premised on a definitive full-scale realization, there are other conceivable alternatives, such as temporary realization in a less costly material, a portable demountable model, or the choice of a smaller scale, whereby the approximately 20-metre height is reduced to, say, four metres (a scale of 1:5), as opted for by Mick Eekhout [fig. 20]. Such cases, according to architectural historian Manfred Bock, do not entail a reconstruction, but a new format. In his view, the shift in scale signals the model's status as interpretation, thus distancing it from the original model.[30]

A design inspired by the Maison d'Artiste offers yet another design premise. In such an approach, a new, more contemporary rendering takes precedence over a historical interpretation.

For example, an 'interpretation' of the Maison d'Artiste in the Gemeentemuseum in The Hague in 2013 took the form of a cluster of viewing boxes: exhibition designers Kossmann.dejong made a design for multiple cabinets of curiosities, based on the Maison d'Artiste [fig. 104]. In one of the museum galleries they placed a room-sized display case, with set-back and projecting rectangular volumes that referred loosely to the 1923 model. The theme of this project was primarily the art of exhibition itself. But when the balance tips towards the new, the Maison d'Artiste tends to get lost from sight.

104 Kossmann De Jong, Cabinets of Curiosities Exhibition, Gemeentemuseum Den Haag, 2013. The design of the 'Wonderkamers' was based in part on the Maison d'Artiste
Photo Thijs Wolzak

The EFL Stichting believes that a design commission in which a young or internationally prominent architect drew inspiration from the design by Van Doesburg and Van Eesteren could result in an interesting project. In an interview about the possibilities for realization in early 2016, the foundation's chairman, Maurits de Hoog, stated that a phased approach could be adopted for decision-making about a design: 'A first step might be to choose one out of several possible interpretations of the design. One of those options is a strict reconstruction, but it is the least exciting and will always be open to question. That's why other interpretations need to be explored as well. A study commission awarded to various architects – young, international – could be a good way of tackling that.'[31]

Closely related to design considerations is the intended use: 'It would be interesting for instance to gain more insight into temporary or more permanent solutions. A temporary summer pavilion à la the Serpentine Pavilions in London's Hyde Park, imposes different usage requirements than a more long-term operation. It won't be easy to find an appropriate function for a permanent pavilion, without compromising the design.'[32] The future will show how these ideas develop and whether a new synergy emerges between a client, function, design and location for the Maison d'Artiste.

28 For the use of black-and-white photographs for colour reconstruction: Suttorp 1994; Postma 1995, pp. 55-63; Janssen 2012, p. 198.

29 HNI EEST 3.210; and HNI DOES-AB-5130; and CMU APB-5630

30 Bock during a discussion about the buildability of the Maison d'Artiste in 2000, Eekhout 2015, p. 16.

31 The EFL Stichting draws a comparison with a 'licence agreement with an added proviso', of the kind used for the filming of a book, which entails step-by-step progress towards a definitive permission for implementation. Interview with Maurits de Hoog, chairman of the EFL Stichting, 3 March 2016.

32 Interview with Maurits de Hoog, chairman of the EFL Stichting, 3 March 2016.

105 Culture cluster Enschede, SeARCH, 2003–2008. History of the place is embedded in the redevelopment of the Roombeek residential district. For the museum, surviving building fragments were incorporated into the new building.
Photo Christian Richters

Wouter Jan Verheul

# Embedded developments
# The connection between prominent buildings and a place

## Sense of place

A building can make or break a place. But the reverse is also true. A place can allow a building to come into its own and the place can detract from the value of a building. Which is why the relation between place and building is a frequent topic of discussion, especially when the building in question is visually significant. In practice, the relationship between place and building can vary from harmonious and exciting, to disruptive or noncommittal. This chapter examines in more detail the importance and the complexity of the relation between a building and its surroundings. Using insights from sociology, planning and public administration, the relation between place and building is further elucidated, supported by examples of contested or commended architectural projects. The key idea is that a 'sense of place' is essential. Hence the argument that image-defining buildings should be embedded in the local setting.

## Between building and place

The question of whether a building fits into its surroundings is related to form, style and taste, to the past and the future. And the question concerns both the interests of the parties involved, who stand to gain from a building, and the interests of those who are likely to be disadvantaged by it. It is a question that merits the attention of initiators and designers, whether it concerns a location in search of a new and fitting design, as in the construction of a new concert hall and dance theatre on Spuiplein in The Hague, or an existing design in search of a location, as in the case of the Maison d'Artiste, the design by De Stijl members Theo van Doesburg and Cornelis van Eesteren, the realization options for which have been explored by various parties for over ten years now. The question of whether something suits a particular location is sometimes the subject of passionate public debate that may even drag on for years. In Almere, for example, the debate about completing a building project in the form of a medieval castle [fig. 106], has been going on for over fifteen years. According to opponents, a retro castle would be out of place in this modernist new town.

The significance of buildings and places is to a large degree socially constructed. That is certainly true of projects of a public nature. A designer, developer or administrator may have exalted ideas about the value of a new architectural project, but the way a building is used, is appropriated, is integrated into the urban fabric, is embraced, cherished and is part of local pride and self-awareness, ultimately depends on how a wide-ranging group of users experience it and the significance they attach to it.[1]

The relation between object and place is an important element of a design task, in the wider sense of the word. The spatial planner Varkki George distinguishes between 'first-order' and 'second-order' design.[2] 'First-order design is about the (physical) design tasks of a project, 'second-order design' is about organizing the decision-making environment within which the various actors operate. Think here of architects, developers and administrators, supporters and opponents, the social world of residents and the systems world of decision makers. 'Second-order design' determines the context in which the 'first-order design' takes place. In other words, the success of a physical design of a building and a place – the relation between them – also depends on the way the process in which the actors are involved is organized.

## Globalization and rootless architecture

Is that relation between building and place always so well-considered and present? When we look at the development of our urban landscape in recent decades, maybe not at all. 'Everything in the built environment looks more and more the

1 Verheul 2012.
2 George 1997.

same', is a constant refrain.[3] It seems as if the same shopping streets, office buildings and street furniture pop up everywhere. How does that uniformity come about? There are several possible explanations.

The uniform environment is partly the result of improved transport options and increasing industrialization, which have delivered many economies of scale during the past one hundred years. Like popular merchandise, the built environment has undergone a process of uniformity and commodification, resulting in objectification and alienation. The uniformity of the built environment is also linked to the advent and ubiquity of multinational enterprises, which impose their uniform house style on facades and interiors all over the world, because they feel that, in the interests of recognizability and predictability, a retail and product experience should be the same everywhere. The sociologist George Ritzer called this process the 'McDonaldization of society'.[4] Thanks to the uniformity of products, services and the physical environment, every form of local identity disappears, culminating in a 'globalization of nothing'.[5]

The built environment is also dominated by big banks, insurance companies, technology corporations and other international service providers. Architecturally speaking these multinationals tend to have similar stylistic preferences and often choose the same architects of international name and fame, who are wont to produce 'context-less' designs.[6] Pension funds and other real estate investors are keen to rent their properties to multinationals because of the long-term financial security. This is an insidious process of globalization by multinationals, or 'a silent takeover' as the economist Noreena Hertz (2002) has dubbed it. The consequence is social alienation and a privately controlled urban space where an individual is never genuinely free because private parties have a say in who may come there, how they behave and what they say.[7]

Thus globalization poses a potential threat both to the physical local identity and to social cohesion, democracy and the influence of the local population. This can lead to estrangement, to buildings and places that are no longer about people, but have degenerated into anonymous, uncaring spaces.

## Glocalization and sense of place

Must we then conclude that increasing globalization leads to the disappearance of place and local identity? 'The world is flat', wrote the economist and journalist Thomas Friedman in 2005 in his book of the same name. If the Internet, smartphones and other ICT applications enable us to work, acquire information and keep in touch with one another wherever we may be, why should place matter anymore? We spend a great deal of our time in a global virtual environment.

But if one looks further, one finds that there is most certainly a demand for distinctive places. Precisely because we are able to work and exchange information anywhere and everywhere from in front of a screen, we want to be able to choose which surroundings we prefer to be in. Place, in its physical, social and cultural manifestations, really does matter. The connection we experience in a place, is also known as a 'sense of place', whereby 'sense' means 'feeling', 'meaning' and 'sensory faculty'. 'Sense of place' can be interpreted as a 'total sensory experience'; we can as it were hear, smell and taste a place.[8] The mere thought of New York evokes the sound of honking taxis, and we can already smell the salt sea air as soon as we book a holiday in a seaside resort. 'Sense of place' is an important happiness factor for people, according to research conducted by the sociologist Richard Florida (2008). Based on a survey carried out among ten thousand people, Florida ranked the things that made them happy. And what did it show? Right at the top were personal relationships and loved ones, followed by the place where one lived – higher even than income. In other words, most people derive greater happiness from the place where they live than from the salary they receive.

In recent years, globalization has been counter-balanced by a development that is also known as 'glocalization'. One example is the current popularity of food from one's own region. More and more people want to know where their food comes from and appreciate products that come with a story about the maker and the place of origin. Local products are emerging that simultaneously meet global standards. This 'return of the local' is also evident in other product groups. In some places a 'Local First' network develops, made up of independent small to medium retailers, such as supermarkets, bookshops or coffee bars, which sell local products or operate independently of international chains. The products and services offered may never be one hundred per cent local, but they do integrate local and international products. According to George Ritzer: 'the glocalization of something offers at least some hope for cultural heterogeneity in a world in which the truly local has almost entirely disappeared.'[9]

Parallel with the re-evaluation of local products, we also see a growing demand for buildings with a local and historically embedded narrative. The character and history of existing buildings are valued as a guideline for redevelopment.[10] In that respect, glocalization and 'sense of place' have important implications for the way we view relationships between buildings and places.

106 Almere Castle, Penta architecten, Almere-Haven, 1999. The architects modelled the amenities centre on a Belgian castle of medieval origins. Critics claim that the (still) unfinished complex is out of place in the modernist new town.
Photo Penta Architecten

## Embedded development of the built environment

How can we take the 'sense of place' into account in the development of buildings and places? In other words, how can we avoid developing unresponsive projects, buildings that have no relationship with the surroundings? How can we design and develop in such a way that the buildings and the places are in the limelight while at the same time users feel a connection with the 'place'? My own research (2012) suggests that there are several relevant principles, which can be illustrated with reference to a few cases. These principles can be applied to places where there is a need for new construction, but also to existing designs in search of a location, like the Maison d'Artiste design, for which a succession of sites – Rotterdam, Nagele, The Hague and Amsterdam (Oosterdok) – have been considered in recent years, but which has so far failed to find the right locale. But it can also be helpful to look at other never realized project designs that have for one reason or another aroused the interest of (potential) clients or developers.

The central idea behind these principles is the 'architecture of embedded renewal', which is to say: glocalization applied to the design of the built environment.[11] Embedded renewal is not about a nostalgic yearning for retro architecture, but about design that seeks out contemporary preferences, linked to the local identity and history; about the addition of new elements embedded in the local.

The development of a connection between building and place begins with *acquiring knowledge* about the spatial, social and economic characteristics of a place, identifying the *genius loci*. This concerns both the 'facts' and the 'feelings' of a place. According to public administration expert Nico Nelissen (2003), the designer needs to 'know the spirit of a place in order to be able to provide an architectural response to it'.[12] That knowledge can be used in deciding on functions and the design of buildings and places. The team designing the new Roombeek residential area in Enschede, for example, studied the economic and spatial planning history of the area devastated by a fireworks disaster in May 2000, and used this in planning its reconstruction. Existing buildings were integrated into new designs and 'bleaching fields' from the textile era returned in a surprising form [fig. 105]. Room was also found for the long-established self-build culture. Allowing owner-built housing resulted in a heterogeneous mix of historical and modern styles. For tourists and residents of the new Roombeek alike, the reborn district tells a unique Enschede story.

3 Spierings 2006; Zukin 2010.
4 Ritzer 1993.
5 Ritzer 2007.
6 Sklair 2006.
7 Lehning 2001.
8 Hospers 2013.
9 Ritzer 2003, p. 189.
10 Steenhuis and Meurs 2012.
11 Verheul 2013a.
12 Nelissen 2003, p. 24.

## Design principles for embedded renewal

Several design principles are important for binding building and place together, including the *reinterpretation of locally existing forms*. For example, the architect Liesbeth van der Pol used the high tension masts and grain silos dotting the polder landscape as a frame of reference in designing three apartment towers (the so-called Red Devils) in Almere [fig. 107]. In Eindhoven the huge cohort of steel columns at the entrance to the covered

107 Rooie Donders apartments, DOK Architecten, 1994–1998, Almere-Buiten. The design of the apartment towers refers to the grain silos and old industrial buildings in the vicinity, so that they mark the urban periphery in a meaningful way.
Photo Rob 't Hart

108 Piazza Center Eindhoven, Massimiliano Fuksas, 2004. The steel structure of the covered shopping centre evokes associations with the medieval Woensel Gate that once stood on this spot.
Photo Norbert van Onna

Piazza shopping centre [fig. 108] refer to a medieval city gate (the Oud-Woenselse Poort), which had been excavated a few metres away. Although the personal tastes of people viewing these buildings will differ, they demonstrate that the designers have tried to counteract uniformity by using local formal references.

Things are rather more difficult with pre-existing designs in search of a location, like the Maison d'Artiste. In such cases, the process of including local characteristics in the design is only possible in retrospect. Apart from the commercial prospects, which must be favourable, the design principles that apply to new plans are equally important in existing plans, including connecting the function, the use, the (public) space around a building and the physical connectivity (infrastructure) with surrounding neighbourhoods. The questions that then arise are: was the design intended for a specific place? Was there an envisaged function? Do forms and materials refer to a particular place or region? And can that relationship still be created or strengthened?

It is evident that the *function* of buildings and places must match the needs of initiators and users. A public function for an image-defining building usually increases the likelihood of local acceptance. During the past ten years, the Almere city council has rejected new-start plans for the aforementioned Almere Castle from a development party keen to turn what was originally designed as a wedding venue and leisure centre into apartments. In the council's judgement a public function is desirable on the castle location. Especially in places perceived as part of the public domain, buildings with a public function are more appropriate than private, closed infills.

A building's significance for a place also depends on the

*catalysing ambitions and strategies* – the question of to what extent the building acts as an economic catalyst for the surrounding area. To generate synergy effects, for example, new museums are added to existing museum clusters, as in the MuseumsQuartier in Vienna. Public projects may also be developed with the aim of revitalizing (disadvantaged) neighbourhoods via the influx of visitors and the money they spend in the local shops and restaurants. The effect of the new museum on the Bowery in New York is an example of this process, which is also known as 'culture-led regeneration'.[13] But flywheel effects rarely happen spontaneously; catalytic ambitions call for a careful implementation strategy if the surrounding area is truly to profit.[14]

The catalyst effect is partly determined by the *connectivity of roads and other infrastructure.* The EYE Film Museum in Amsterdam and the surrounding new Overhoeks residential area are clearly visible across the water from Central Station, but if the location is to have a greater impact on the surrounding areas of Amsterdam-Noord, the physical connections will need to be improved. It is currently still too much of an enclave, not least because of the canal separating Overhoeks from the adjacent Van der Pek neighbourhood. In addition, the public space around the EYE is more of an efficient transition zone for museum visitors than a recreational social space for other city users [fig. 109]. Embedded development calls for a design of the *public space* that welcomes diverse and local use.[15]

109 EYE Film museum, Delugan Meissl, Amsterdam, 2010–2012. The waterside location generates a social space with a strong character, but also creates an enclave.
Photo Erwin Zijlstra

## Dialogue with the environs

As stated at the beginning of this chapter, the design task of creating a link between building and place is twofold: in addition to the physical aspect ('first-order design'), it is also necessary to embed the actors in the local context ('second-order design'). Embedded project development entails literally engaging in a dialogue with the surroundings. In *Brandscapes*, architect and publicist Anna Klingmann argues that architectural projects should

13 Gonzalez and Guadiana 2013.
14 Verheul 2013b.
15 See, among others: www.pps.org and Gehl 2010.

not just stand out in their surroundings, but should more particularly act as cultural links between groups of people, between the global market and the local place, between public and private parties.[16] Such an ambition means creating an environment for new projects in which diverse groups are invited to contribute to the planning. 'Placemaking' that respects local identity can only come about after an intensive, open dialogue between different voices in the community.[17]

Despite the Dutch tradition of seeking public input, policy implementers often regard involving the local community as too complicated and time-consuming. The reason why a plan for a football stadium in Rotterdam was cancelled by the city council in 2014 was partly to do with the fact that the stadium management had avoided the conversation with the population, despite the fact that it was asking for financial guarantees from the public purse.[18] Ignoring the neighbourhood can not only frustrate the realization process further down the track, it is also a missed opportunity. The involvement of various actors is more than a democratic virtue or an electoral necessity; it is also a way of taking advantage of local creativity.[19] A broadly supported narrative binding building and place can only emerge if this has been developed step by step with a diverse group of local participants.[20]

## The embedding of participating actors

How can a network of relevant actors be identified and used in the development of projects? According to public administration experts Eric-Hans Klijn and Joop Koppenjan, there are several steps involved, beginning with identifying the most obvious actors.[21] In this case, developers, financiers, government authorities, local residents, cultural institutions, social organizations, interest groups and the media. The initial views on a project are usually the product of a few passionate individuals and a circle of followers, but it is important not to lose sight of people and groups who do not belong to existing networks. The latter often turn out to be overly homogeneous, while other players and new informal networks can prove to be very valuable.

To reach a consensus about the elaboration of a building in a particular place, it is advisable to gain an understanding of the viewpoints, interests and resources of the relevant actors and also to identify mutual relationships and their nature. Is there evidence of harmony or conflict, of obstacles in existing processes or possible barriers? Apart from being conversant with the legal and institutional aspect – for example, environmental regulations or municipal decision-making procedures – process facilitators would be well advised to find out about the informal contacts between the actors. The resolution of substantive differences of opinion between actors lies not only in the cognitive, but often also in the social sphere, according to public administration research.[22]

If actors are invited to have a say about a project initiative, a few process conditions are necessary.[23] First and foremost, openness: everyone who wants to contribute is welcome, no idea is automatically wrong and there must be transparency regarding the chosen process of consultation and decision-making. It is also important that parties feel that their core values are recognized and safeguarded. If parties know that their core values are protected, they will be more willing to adapt particular viewpoints or to seek synergy. A good example is the development of the High Tech Campus in Eindhoven where the Philips group eventually managed to get the city council and the regional environmental organization (Brabantse Milieufederatie) to accept its proposal to build an office development in the green environment of the Dommel Valley. After the Milieufederatie had opposed an office park, Philips initiated a process aimed at modifying the plans and strengthening the ecological diversity of the intended site. The campus became greener, with more space for recreation, and was also opened up to the general public. Physical local values were embedded in the design for the project [fig. 110].

Project initiatives that manage to connect with the more deep-seated values of the actors and with the social discourse about places, have enormous potential. This assumes being mindful of a wide range of groups and their stories. Thus the embedded development of building projects is not just a matter of bricks and mortar, but also of building narrative coalitions and alliances. That implies building on stories about buildings and places in which people recognize themselves; stories that are connected with sense of place.

110 High Tech Campus, Juurlink [+] Geluk, Eindhoven, 2009. The landscape provided the inspiration for the design of the public space of the business park. The park increases the opportunities for recreation of the people who work there and is also open to the general public.
Photo Juurlink [+] Geluk Stedenbouw en Landschap

**16** Klingmann 2007.
**17** Healey 2010.
**18** Van Duijn and Verheul 2015.
**19** Surowiecki 2004.
**20** Verheul and Daamen 2014.
**21** Klijn & Koppenjan 2004.
**22** Termeer 2007.
**23** Bruijn, Ten Heuvelhof, In 't Veld, 2010.

111 C.R. Mackintosh, M. MacDonald (design 1901), A. MacMillan (realization of design 1989), House for an Art Lover, Glasgow. Mackintosh's design was finally realized over 90 years after it was conceived, using the original drawings but with a different function and in part with a new interior.
Photo House for an Art Lover

Paul Meurs

# Unbuilt 'restored' Restoration, reconstruction and late realizations of modern heritage

## Restoration, reconstruction and late realizations

The notion of finally building Theo van Doesburg and Cornelis van Eesteren's Maison d'Artiste almost one hundred years after it was designed, is unusual but not unique. There are other examples of initially unrealized plans being built many years after the design date or even posthumously. Even more common is the practice of rebuilding destroyed buildings or disfigured monuments. If an unrealized design is many years later modified to suit a different location, current legislation, specific user needs or construction-related possibilities, this amounts to a new design, based on the original plan. The result is a cross between a restoration and a simulation. In practice ideas regarding late realization bear strong similarities to 'normal' restoration practice. Judgements about authenticity, trustworthiness and structural detailing are related. This chapter places the phenomenon of late realization in the context of the treatment of modern heritage and of international examples of late realizations.

## Material authenticity

Were the Maison d'Artiste indeed to be realized, the initiators would give due consideration to the quest for the most authentic possible implementation of the original design. The heritage world is dominated by two long-standing interpretations of authenticity. In the first, heritage is seen as a product of its own history, including renovations, additions and wear and tear. Everything about an unrestored building is authentic – it is devoid of later interpretations or corrections. This form of authenticity focuses on the material substance: the age value, the patina of time and the history of use. The untouched material reveals, now and in the future, the history of the structure. The monument is from that perspective its own archive and has value as a historical source. Later on, using as yet unknown techniques, research can be carried out into the original source material (for example, old beams, layers of paint, wallpaper) without being hampered by restorations or because authentic material has ended up in a builder's skip.

The interpretation of authenticity that is linked to the material substance belongs to the heritage practice of forbearance and non-intervention. And that can often prove frustrating, for recent renovations – such as laths, orange bathroom tiles, suspended ceilings and plastic frames introduced at a later date – are wont to obscure our view of what remains of previous phases, while that is usually what we value most. Many restoration specialists consequently find it difficult to practise forbearance. Their hands itch to expose the hidden layers of a building. Once that has been done, they are able, based on the results of the building research, information from the archives, historical illustrations and their knowledge of historical construction, to arrive at an interpretation of the construction history. That is the prelude to the restoration concept: a design, based on what remains of the existing condition and the insights provided by the research.

## Conceptual authenticity

Restoration, in the sense of designing with history, furnishes the second form of authenticity. This is not so much geared to the conservation of the original fabric, but to revealing, completing or reconstructing the idea behind the heritage structure. Authenticity refers in this case to the design value and conceptual authenticity, whereby the experience (space, texture, light, movement) is more important than the source value or the age value. What matters is the concept – the spatial manifestation and the selection (from this perspective) of crucial phases in the history of the building's usage and construction history.

Restoration is more or less 'design by research': an interpretation of a heritage structure. It is consequently a product of present-day culture, a reflection of how people interpret and construct the past at a given point in time. In Paramaribo in the 1950s and '60s, for example, the richly decorated wooden houses were carefully measured and partially restored. Today, the research carried out at that time tells us how European building styles and traditions were adapted overseas and acquired their own distinctive rendering. Nowadays, in light of new opinions, we would probably emphasize different aspects, paying more attention to indications of the social, cultural and economic life of those colonial times. In that context, the backyards, where the interaction between different sections of the population evolved, are more important than the stylistic features of the front part of the house. Those yards, with their organic development, were unthinkingly cleaned up and wholly built on decades ago. The story they could have told us can never be fully recovered.[1]

In the heritage world there is an almost constant plea to keep monuments in their current state, which is articulated in the famous motto 'preservation before renovation'.[2] Practice often reveals the reverse. There are always reasons or interests that lead to a historically evolved monument being drastically altered and making way for a (partial) interpretation. Design and perception trump conservation and non-intervention. In recent years a paradoxical situation has arisen. We are very attached to the sense of (material) authenticity, witness the fashion for chipping walls bare in order to expose all the usage traces and alterations. We insist that our decisions be well-founded, in other words that interventions are based on scientific research. Yet at the same time we subject our heritage to everything that the Charter of Venice (1964) and all those other conventions on restoration have expressly forbidden: relocation, compilation of fragments, reconstruction, simulation.[3] Our motivation is the desire to realize a certain perception of a monument. This is backed by the conviction that we can bring back the past in a responsible manner – as if it were makeable.[4]

112 Gerrit Rietveld, Rietveld-Schröder House, Utrecht, photo c. 2009. The interior after the restorations in the 1970s and '80s to a design by Bertus Mulder
Photo Jannes Linders

113 Gerrit Rietveld, Rietveld-Schröder House, Utrecht, photo c. 2009. The outer facade after the restorations in the 1970s and '80s to a design by Bertus Mulder
Photo Jannes Linders

## Conservation through reconstruction

When it comes to the architectural heritage of the Modern Movement, it seems that in many instances the patina, the historical dimension and the imperfections of the experimental construction do not weigh so heavily.[5] Interventions restore the original condition, as if the buildings had never been modified or suffered wear and tear. And as if the designers were still alive and well. An interesting example of this free restoration approach is the Rietveld-Schröder House (1924) in Utrecht. In the 1970s and '80s everything that had made the house famous was stripped and reconstructed: the interior, the stuccoed walls on the exterior and the entire colour palette [figs. 112, 113].[6] Only the core of the house was spared, but that was precisely the part that the original architect, Gerrit Rietveld, had tried to hide away: brick external walls and timber upper floors. Bertus Mulder, the restoration architect, based his design on his experience as Rietveld's assistant and his long-running collaboration with Truus Schröder. That the conceptual reinterpretation of the Rietveld-Schröder House was not seen as a

114 Jan Duiker and Bernard Bijvoet, Zonnestraal Sanatorium, Hilversum. Main building after the restoration by H.J. Henket and W. de Jonge in 2003. Photo Jannes Linders

problem from the heritage viewpoint is evident from the building's later nomination for Unesco's World Heritage list, for which authenticity is a precondition. It underscores the precedence given to conceptual authenticity (design value) when dealing with modern architecture.[7]

In terms of the drastic approach to the fabric of the building, the restoration of the Zonnestraal sanatorium in Hilversum resembles the intervention in the Rietveld-Schröder House. This complex was designed by Jan Duiker and Bernard Bijvoet with the first pavilion being opened for use in 1928. Renovations, neglect and decay had left the complex in such a dilapidated state that during restoration the main building was peeled back to the slender concrete frame, after which the shell was reinstated and refinished. The aim was to restore to perfection the way the building had looked in 1931. Thanks to the original contract drawings, an in-depth, years-long study of the construction history, research into the complex and analysis of old photographs, this proved to be eminently possible.[8] Nevertheless, the restoration (1999–2003) was not a literal reconstruction because numerous physical, structural and other modifications were made. Using contemporary know-how and techniques, it was possible to improve and perpetuate the original intentions of the architects. The result was a newly designed and materialized building with the 'perfect looks' of 75 years earlier [fig. 114]. Where it differs from the Schröder House is that since its construction, the sanatorium had been unrecognizably altered and was in a dilapidated state, whereas until the restoration the Schröder House had known uninterrupted use by the first occupant.

Conservation through reconstruction has also been applied to other listed Nieuwe Bouwen period buildings, such as Rietveld's Sonsbeek Pavilion in the Kröller–Müller Museum. Intended originally as a temporary exhibition building in Arnhem in 1955, it had soon afterwards been dismantled. In 1965 it was rebuilt in Otterlo, a year after Rietveld's death.[9] During the demolition in 2010, the building fabric of that (second) pavilion was analysed in a process of 'destructive research', after which the reconstruction design, by Bertus Mulder, combined insights into the old condition in with structural and other modifications and improvements.[10]

The step from 'conservation through reconstruction' to 'reconstruction of vanished heritage buildings' is considerable. There is after all no longer any existing condition to serve as starting point for the design. A monument must be reassembled,

1 Ozinga 1961; Temminck and Groll 1973; Aarsen and Meurs 2009.

2 Stroux and Quist 2011, p. 5.

3 The international Carter of Venice outlines principles for dealing with restoration and conservation of ensembles and monuments of cultural-historical value; drawn up in Venice in 1964.

4 Meurs 2008.

5 Meurs 2016, p. 40.

6 For notes on the restorations in 1974 (exterior), 1978 (garden), 1985 (interior) written by the restoration architect himself see: Van Zijl and Mulder 2009, pp. 68-93.

7 The restoration history of the Rietveld-Schröder House is the subject of academic research from an architectural-historical perspective being carried out by Marie-Thérèse van Thoor (TU Delft), as part of the project 'Colour, Form and Space: Rietveld Schröder House Challenging the Future' conducted by TU Delft and the Centraal Museum Utrecht, financed by the J.P. Getty Foundation's Keeping it Modern programme (2015).

8 De Jonge 2010.

9 Van Kooten and Bloemheuvel 2007, pp. 330-332; Meurs 2016, p. 70.

10 Van Bommel 2009; see also Mulder 2011.

based purely on historical sources. Once again there are many examples in modern architecture, including Ludwig Mies van der Rohe's Barcelona Pavilion (1929, rebuilt 1986), Le Corbusier's Pavillon de l'Esprit Nouveau in Paris (1925, rebuilt in Bologna 1977) and in the Netherlands, the facade of café De Unie (1924, rebuilt 1986) and the construction site office for the Oud-Mathenesse housing estate (1923, rebuilt 1993), both by J.J.P. Oud in Rotterdam.[11] With the exception of the Barcelona Pavilion, all entailed reconstruction in a new location.[12]

## Unbuilt 'restored'

Realization of unbuilt monuments is the next step along the spectrum of the restoration and reconstruction of cultural heritage. Given that it is not possible to refer to an actual or vanished material reality, this can be seen as 'conceptual realization'. A concept, recorded in a drawing, model, written notes or specifications, is the starting point. Depending on how much time has elapsed between design and realization and how detailed the original design is, the elaboration into a buildable design will, to a lesser or greater degree, amount to a new interpretation.

The longer the period between design and realization, the more one can speak of a new design or a conceptual realization. With the passing of the years, circumstances change. The original designer and client have departed the scene. The location changes. There are new rules and regulations, different building materials, new building products (while old ones have disappeared from the market) and the function often changes as well. A classic case is an unrealized design from around 1732 by Daniël Marot (1661–1752) for a baroque garden at Huis ten Bosch in The Hague. This garden was realized centuries later as part of a theme park in Nagasaki.[13] The garden design can be enjoyed in combination with a reconstruction of Huis ten Bosch – and the result is a unique, authentic experience.

Owing to the emphasis on conceptual authenticity, non-realized designs of modern architecture are popular candidates for late realization. Among connoisseurs, some unrealized plans enjoy iconic status. Initiators of late realizations appropriate that status by making something new that is already firmly established in the collective memory (of the professional community) and may even be world renowned. The model, the 3D spectacles and cinematic computer animations cannot be compared with the experience and the emotion that a built concept is able to generate.

## Conceptual restorations

The model of the Maison Dom-Ino by Le Corbusier (1887–1965) on the site of the Venice Biennale (1915, built 2014) can be regarded as a realized concept [fig. 115]. For practical reasons, this realization was executed in wood. According to the latter-day designers, the wooden model reveals three of the original principles: the use of prefabricated elements assembled on the spot; a basic shell that can be finished locally; and the use of a unit that can be repeated horizontally (and perhaps even vertically).[14] The implementation looks rather bare because it is just a shell with no cladding or walls. Now that Le Corbusier's sketches have been realized there remains little scope for the imagination. The added value of this conceptual realization is that the dimensions and scale of this iconic design are now apparent – the shell looks smaller than one would have expected.

115 Le Corbusier, Maison Dom-Ino, design 1915, realization in 2014 by the Architectural Association School of Architecture London for the Venice Biennale. The light and demountable timber construction of the full-scale realization makes the building suitable to travel (photo 2014)
Photo Paul Meurs

In 2013, the Belgian architects Robbrecht & Daem built an unrealized 1930 design by Mies van der Rohe (1886–1969) for a golf clubhouse in Krefeld.[15] As a basis for their reinterpretation they had some eighty design drawings by Mies at their disposal, including an 'endgültige Zustand' (definitive situation).[16] This reconstruction was executed as a temporary pavilion, a full-scale model, which gives the impression of a gigantic maquette [figs. 116, 117]. Here, too, the size (in this case immense) was perceptible.

The model also makes it possible to experience the relation between the architecture and the landscape in the open-plan spaces. What is missing is the material and the detail, and that is not insignificant for a work by the architect who was famous for his dictum: ‘God is in the details’. The temporary building lacks the richness and the godlike precision that is, however, present in the reconstructed Barcelona Pavilion. The clubhouse illustrates what a mock-up can and cannot achieve. If the Barcelona approach had been followed for the new realization in Krefeld, and Mies van der Rohe’s characteristic detailing and materialization had been taken as starting point, then maybe the designer’s genius would have come to life here as well. But of course that was not the intention of the Belgian architects and the budget probably would not have stretched that far either.[17]

In a similar vein to the Barcelona Pavilion is the Wall House by John Hejduk (1929–2000) in Groningen. This American architect made his mark with a series of conceptual designs, a kind of architectural etudes. Around the time when the Wall House series was designed (1973), there was a client, the landscape architect A.E. Bye, and a location, in Ridgefield (Connecticut), for the second variant. But in the event, it was never built. Years later Hejduk was in Groningen in connection with the Stadsmarkering project (1990) and a (never realized) housing project in the city centre. Along the way the idea was born to build Wall House #2 in Groningen as homage to Hejduk.[18] The icon was transplanted to a new housing estate as a form of differentiation and spatial identity. Hejduk was enthusiastic about the initiative but did not live to see its completion in 2000. Unlike the Maison Dom-Ino in Venice and the full-scale model of the clubhouse in Krefeld, the Wall House in Groningen is more than an architectural idea solidified in matter. It is a fully fledged building, congenial, occupied and integrated into the landscape of the Hoornse Meer district [fig. 118].

The last late realization examined here is the House for an Art Lover, a 1901 competition entry by Charles Rennie Mackintosh

116 Golf Club, Krefeld. Realization of temporary pavilion designed by Robbrecht en Daem in 2013. Original design by Ludwig Mies van der Rohe, 1930. The exposed timber supporting structure emphasizes the temporariness of the pavilion. Robbrecht en Daem architecten / photo Thomas Hick

117 Golf Club, Krefeld. Realization of temporary pavilion designed by Robbrecht en Daem in 2013. Original design by Ludwig Mies van der Rohe, 1930 Robbrecht en Daem architecten / photo Thomas Hick

11 Another project by J.J.P. Oud, De Kiefhoek housing estate, was demolished and rebuilt to a design by Wytze Patijn. Overmeiere and Patijn 1990.

12 In Eindhoven initiators have been trying since 2006 to rebuild the Philips Pavilion that was on show at the World’s Fair in Brussels in 1958. The Alice Foundation (2006), and since 2013 the Foundation for the Reconstruction of the 1958 Philips Pavilion. Wever 2015, pp. 148-149.

13 Meurs 1992.

14 The assembly of wooden elements makes the design suitable for travelling. Design by vbvb studio, Valentin Bontjes van Beek, realized by the Architectural Association School of Architecture, London. Koolhaas 2014, pp. 184-185, pp. 384-385.

15 Dannenmann 2014.

16 Lange 2014, p. 72

17 Lange et al. 2014.

18 Martin and Smals, 2001.

(1868–1928) and Margaret MacDonald (1864–1933).[19] It was not until 1989 that it was finally built, over a period of seven years, in a park in Glasgow [figs. 111, 119].[20] In the late realization the original residential function was changed to a gallery, shop and conference space. Mackintosh had detailed the exterior and part of the interior in perspective drawings. These, in combination with other built work by the architect, made it possible to arrive at a faithful interpretation (architect Andy MacMillan). The

118 John Hejduk, Wall House, realized in 2001 in Groningen. Based on one of the variants in the Wall House series of 1973, which the American architect designed for a location in Ridgefield (Connecticut). Photo Christian Richters

'authentic' interior is confined to the spaces drawn by Mackintosh (double-height hall, dining room, music room and oval room), complemented with a staircase and a gallery. This totality is known as the Mackintosh Suite. For the elaboration of the gallery, the architect was able to draw on comparable elements in Windyhill (1899–1901), a realized villa design by Mackintosh. The reconstruction of the House for an Art Lover shows not only that a design can be built generations after the fact, but also how important it is to know how far to go with reconstruction. The foundation that manages the house is conscious of the dilemmas surrounding authenticity. Mackintosh's sketch designs are displayed in every room so that visitors are always able to form their own opinion on Mackintosh's design and the later interpretation.

## Variations on Van Doesburg and Van Eesteren

The initiative to build the Maison d'Artiste designed by Theo van Doesburg and Cornelis van Eesteren has something in common with the realization of the House for an Art Lover. In both cases the ambition is to make a complete structure, based on an incomplete design. In Glasgow it entailed a step from Provisional Design to Definitive Design. In the case of the Maison d'Artiste there is not even a complete Provisional Design. Van Doesburg and Van Eesteren made a maquette (of which only black-and-white photographs exist) and a few sketches. There are no specifications, indeed it is unclear what the building was supposed to look like inside – which colours should have gone where (not unimportant for Van Doesburg's oeuvre), and how the construction design was conceived.

To turn this incomplete design into a building, several approaches are possible. First of all, the restoration architect could try to 'put himself in Van Doesburg's shoes' and take an imaginary journey back to 1923. Thus he could complete the design in a simulation of what would have been possible in those days. The challenge here is to remain faithful both to the thinking of the original designers and to the state of construction and technology back then. The second approach also involves putting oneself in the position of Van Doesburg and Van Eesteren, but then bringing them along into the present day as it were. In this way current materials, computational methods and structural possibilities become available – and it's a moot point what Van Doesburg and Van Eesteren would have been able to do with them. The outcome will undoubtedly have the alienating effect of an anachronism. Who is the author? What is authentic? Will it be a spectacular design that is layered in time, or conversely a banal rip-off of a once avant-garde design, a desperate retro-modernism? The third option for realizing the incomplete design is to construct everything that is known about the building and to omit everything that is lacking. This results in an inaccessible reconstruction, a monolith that can be experienced as a powerful De Stijl icon, without this image being eroded by later interpretations or additions. The fourth and final option is to build the distance in time into the reconstruction and to maintain a distinction between Van Doesburg and Van Eesteren (then) and the necessary additions (now). This duality provides the freedom to make a contemporary building independently of the original designers, a building that can relate freely to the 1923 design. It will be difficult enough to come up with a convincing exterior.

Uncertainty about the colour application advocated by Van Doesburg, may well translate into an installation in which the building changes colour like a chameleon and thus makes it possible to experience different interpretations of the colour design. The realizations in Nagasaki, Venice, Krefeld, Groningen and Glasgow underscore the freedom offered by a conceptual restoration when an existing condition is absent. One is free to opt for a shell, a full-size model, a simulation, or an elaboration

119 C.R. Mackintosh, M. MacDonald (design 1901), A. MacMillan (realization of design 1989), House for an Art Lover, Glasgow. For the realization of the music room the original 1901 drawings were used. Photo Findhorn

into an incomplete, but authentic and credible whole. Different layers of time can be introduced into the realization such that an interpretation of the exterior has a different time dimension from the interior. As long as the incomplete Maison d'Artiste remains unbuilt, everyone can imagine it in their own way. Once the building is there, that will become a good deal more difficult. The challenge of the conceptual realization is to maintain the iconic status of the sketch by Van Doesburg and Van Eesteren and to add something to it. For the completed, layered or simulated building to come across as authentic and credible demands the utmost care. The reconstruction of the Maison d'Artiste can make or break the reputation of the icon.

**19** The construction (1989–1996) was supervised by Andy MacMillan, at that moment head of the architecture course at the Glasgow School of Art. www.houseforanartlover.co.uk (consulted 14 March 2016).

**20** Kaplan 1996, pp. 334-335; Levine 2008, p. 16.

120 Hans Jaffé, *De Stijl 1917-1931. The Dutch contribution to modern art*, 1956. The groundbreaking research by art historian Hans Jaffé formed the basis of the academic study of De Stijl.

Ole Bouman

# Maison d'Artiste
# Nevermore, possibly, or quite soon?

The study of art and culture is part of the spirit of the age. In the early 1980s, for example, the study of art history at the University of Amsterdam was largely dictated by dogma. The compulsory exam material consisted of Marxist pamphlets in which all art was explained in terms of class differences. At the same time, the young members of the faculty were ushering in a new paradigm in which every claim to historical objectivity was exchanged for an equally strong claim to historical relativity. Art was no more than a simulacrum, an illusory world in which the artist became the unresisting interpreter of the postmodern condition. Even art, the domain of imagination and creation, could embody nothing more than the inescapable 'emptiness of the sign'.

In the midst of this ideological game of musical chairs, I – a student of both art history and cultural history – very soon became aware of the rare exceptions. The freethinkers. The curious. One of these was Hans Jaffé (1915–1984), professor of the history of modern art, who had embarked on his swansong as lecturer. There he stood, an old man on the podium of a vast lecture theatre, in front of a brainwashed audience that had been thoroughly prepared during the orientation classes to withstand the nonsense spouted by someone who still believed in art. But Jaffé said very little. For the most part he showed his 'slides'. First of work by Kandinsky and Klee, art as the truth behind reality. Then Van Doesburg and Van Eesteren, their House of the Artist as the habitat of truth. Jaffé had no interest in ideology; he quite simply declared his love. He revealed a truth, not through dogma, but through enquiry.

There was something else about Jaffé that I barely noticed at first. Later on I realized that it was quite exceptional among art historians. He spoke about the characteristics of De Stijl, not as an artistic movement, but as a body of ideas, not as a subjective style of a group of artistic friends or even competitors, but as a sort of rehabilitation of the truth, an expression of a national spiritual character. In short, as something that really mattered. Jaffé showed that the choice between a straight or a diagonal line could be a moral rather than an aesthetic choice. That the use of primary colours or the total mutual permeation of art and architecture had nothing to do with decoration, and everything to do with a view about pure living. Here spoke someone who could empathize with the iconoclastic craving for an environment devoid of all anecdotal carry-on, based in a way of thinking in which an artwork had vanquished the supremely individual in favour of the axiomatic. An artwork seen not as an object, but as a model for a new life and a new society. Maison d'Artiste was not a house *for an artist*, but a house *of the artist* – the kind of artist envisaged by De Stijl. A microcosm to embody the truth.

Can and should this house be built after all this time? Based on an analysis of what once animated its creators, you would have to conclude that such an ambition is well-nigh blasphemous. There is after all precious little of that national spiritual character left. The act of building would by definition be frivolous, because it involves rendering the pure idea material. As if one were to reduce pure content to form, profundity to surface gloss. As if one were to force a metaphor to be literal. Or still worse: present a manifesto of the truth as a lie.

And yet it will certainly happen. A variety of reasons and motives have been marshalled to date. They have been successively canvassed in this book. There is the personal passion of a few individuals who have been fighting for realization for years. There is the touristic motive, which has crowds of visitors already queuing at the door. And then there is the iconic motive of putting completely new cultural initiatives on the map with a unique accommodation.

All these motives can be placed alongside the scenarios for realization outlined in the chapter by Paul Meurs. He has spelled out which reconstruction scenarios are conceivable: the historical theatre approach with a 1923 mise-en-scène, as if nothing has happened since then in building technology. The teleporting approach, which sees Van Doesburg and Van Eesteren transported to the present day to materialize their plans using modern means. The classic archeological approach in which the only parts reconstructed are those that can be traced back to historical sources with 100 per cent certainty. Or there is the support and infill method in which something usable is realized within a shell that recalls the original source.

What all these variants lack, however, is the true essence of the original design: the urgent need to erect a utopian model that would put an irreversible end to the cultural climate of dilettantism, anecdote, compromise and, all right: commerce. As Alied Ottevanger, the author of one the chapters in this book, was able to glean from contemporary correspondence, the intention was quite literally to make a work that would burst upon the scene like a bombshell. A dramatic artistic intervention in an immoral and deceitful world, whereby the artist was not the representative of a style, but of De Stijl. The only Stijl, namely that which celebrates the truth.

The desire to reconstruct this particular manifesto, now, at this time, has a symbolic potential that far transcends the art-historical and structural debate about the pros and cons. Especially if that symbolism is reinforced by the right choice of location and the construction becomes a statement in the surrounding practice of compromise and obscure agendas that besets so much culture and architecture at present. It is quite possible that Van Doesburg and Van Eesteren's sense of urgency will come at precisely the right time. When this monument to the truth is opened (or unveiled, or projected) in a few years, the time will also be ripe for us to fully reacquaint ourselves with the original meaning. Not just as a building, but as a message, of which the future programme will undoubtedly be an important embodiment. Indeed, it is meaning that people will be yearning for. What's more, a new house for the truth may be all people want from now on.

121 Theo van Doesburg and Cornelis van Eesteren, counter-construction of the Maison Particulière in colour, 1923, gouache on collotype. Kröller-Muller Museum, Otterlo

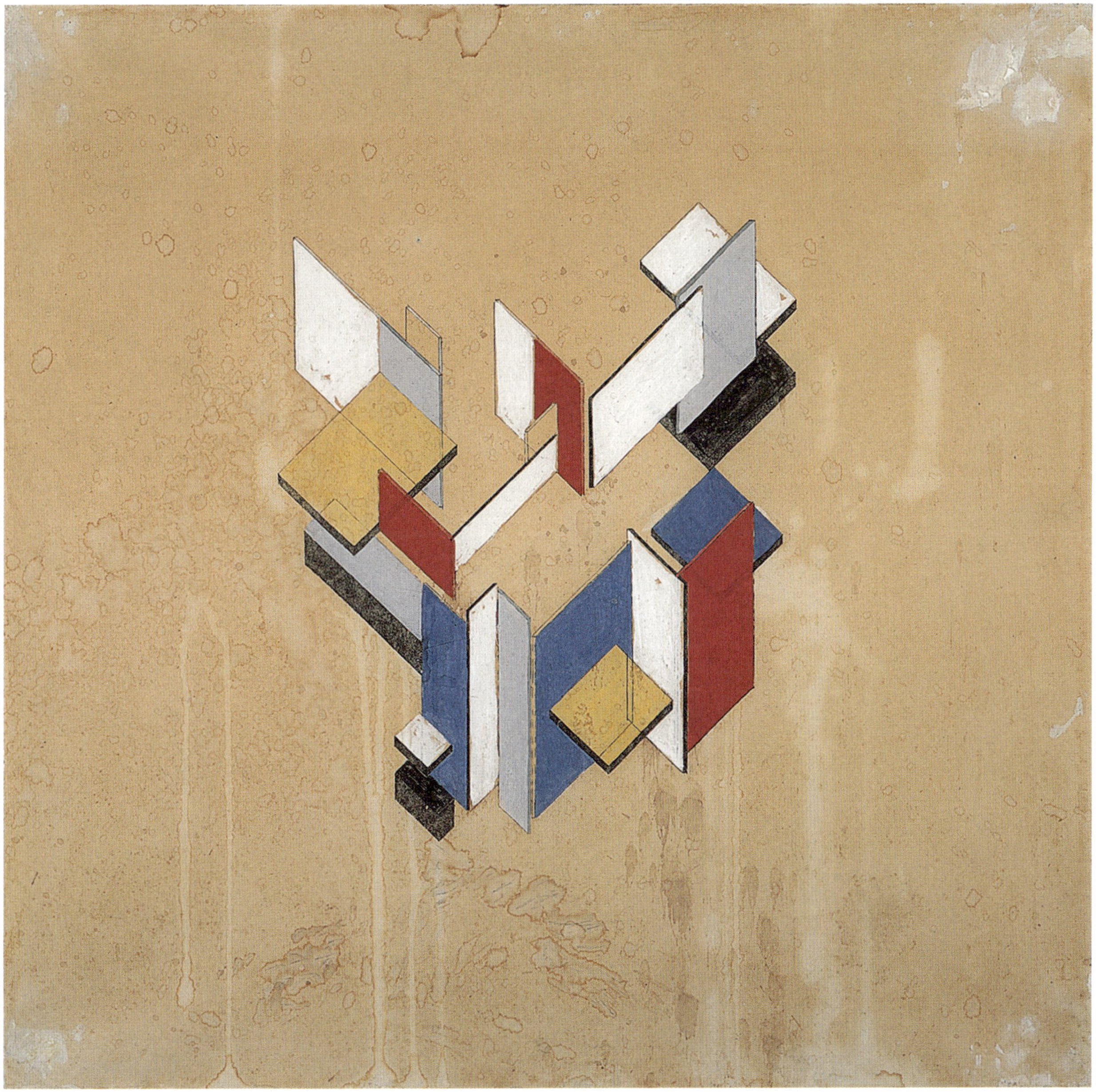

Over the years, numerous designers, artists and others from the cultural sector in the Netherlands and beyond have become involved in various ways in the oeuvre of Theo van Doesburg and Cornelis van Eesteren. Below the reactions of some of them to the possible realization of Maison d'Artiste.

'The design of Maison d'Artiste is of great importance for the development of modern architecture. The incorporated space–time dynamic, derived from the tesseract, finds expression in the spiralled placement of the spaces and the associated application of De Stijl colours. Realization will demonstrate its significance.'

Wies van Moorsel,
art historian, donator of the De Stijl archive and Van Doesburg works to the Dutch state

'From September 1994 to December 1995 Erica Stigter and I lived in Van Doesburg's last house on a hill in Meudon-Val-Fleury, close to Paris. Never before had we experienced space in all its forms, from bold to diffident. If the Maison d'Artiste is finally built, you'll be able to see in your own country how passionately Theo van Doesburg loved space.

K. Schippers,
writer

'If the Maison d'Artiste, after having lived in the imagination for almost a century, were to be realized at last, we would undoubtedly find ourselves in a time warp of sorts. Paradigmatic for De Stijl was an expansive space, which in Mondrian's interior found expression as 'expansion' through 'interiorization', and in the case of Rietveld and Mrs Schröder as 'plasticism' by means of dynamically shifting planes. Will we find ourselves in the Maison d'Artiste within Van Doesburg's 'nouvelle dimension', a tesseract-inspired, stepwise staggered construction that is actively form-shaping, transcends the horizontal orientation and turns time into a three-dimensional element? Only time will tell.'

Marek Wieczorek,
Associate Professor Modern and Contemporary Art history at the University of Washington in Seattle

‘Maison d’Artiste (1923) stands at the juncture of art and architecture. Conceived as a studio space for artists, its volumes are a three dimensional manifestation of a Mondrian painting. It is art as architecture or architecture as art inspiring Rietveld’s Schröder House in Utrecht a year later. There are echoes fifty years later in Moishe Safdie’s “Habitat” apartments built in Montreal, Canada for Expo 67. And now with the publication of this book, Maison d’Artiste continues to inspire us almost a hundred years after it was first conceived.’

Barry R Campbell,
collector, Board Member, Canadian Centre For Architecture

‘Maison d’Artiste is a revolutionary design that has had a lasting effect on modernist architecture. The realized building has the potential to become a monument of the new 20th-century architecture as developed by the avant-garde.’

Sjarel Ex,
director Museum Boijmans Van Beuningen, Rotterdam

‘Dynamism is the key characteristic of modernity. Spatial dynamism, the fourth dimension, is the key characteristic of Maison d’Artiste. It remains a cultural shortcoming as long as this architectural invention has not been realized. It is time for action; the result will be stunning.’

Hubert-Jan Henket,
Honorary President DOCOMOMO International

‘The Maison d’Artiste is an exciting experiment in architectural representation in model form. The creators had grand visions, but in 1923 few opportunities to realize their idea of an all-round, colourful architecture. Just as unfinished symphonies are sometimes finished in the same spirit by someone else at a later date, the architectural model of the Maison d’Artiste is ideally suited to a new, full-scale construction experiment, provided a suitable function can be found for the building, including a yet to be devised appropriate interior.’

Marieke Kuipers,
Professor of Cultural Heritage, Delft Technical University

# Bibliography


Aarsen and Meurs 2009: A. Aarsen and P. Meurs, *De ontwikkelings-potenties van stedelijk werelderfgoed. Een voorbeeldproject in Scharloo Abou, Willemstad*, Delft/Willemstad, 2009

Van Andel 2013: F. van Andel, 'Woningbouw in tijden van crisis/ Housing in Times of Crisis', in: D. van Gameren et al., *Woning-bouwtentoonstellingen/Housing Exhibitions. Delft Architectural Studies on Housing*, Rotterdam 2013, pp. 4-17

Anonymous 1919: 'A Futurist's Idea of a Home', *The Daily Mirror*, 18 November 1919

Anonymous 1920: 'De inrichting der Arbeiderswoning. De tentoon-stelling in het tuindorp', *Voorwaarts* 28 September 1920 (second sheet), p. 56

Anonymous 1923a: 'Nederlandsche kunst te Parijs', *Nieuwe Rotterdamsche Courant*, 19 October 1923

Anonymous 1923b: [W.F.A. Roëll], 'De architecten van De Stijl', *Het Vaderland. Staat- en letterkundig Nieuwsblad*, 20 October 1923

Anonymous 1924a: 'Naar een nieuwen bouwstijl', *Nieuwe Rotterdamsche Courant*, 28 March 1924

Anonymous 1924b: [W.F.A. Roëll], 'Bezoek bij Mondriaan. Het Neo-plasticisme in schilderkunst, bouwkunst, muziek, literatuur', *Het Vaderland. Staat- en letterkundig nieuwsbad*, 17 October 1924

Arpa and Van Andel 2013: J. Arpa and F. van Andel, 'Volgens mij is het 1:1 project een instrument voor debat... Interview met Barry Bergdoll/I Think of the 1:1 Project as a Discursive Tool... Interview with Barry Bergdoll', in: D. van Gameren et al., *Woningbouwtentoonstellingen/Housing Exhibitions. Delft Architectural Studies on Housing*, Rotterdam, pp. 66-72

Arts League Service 1919: Arts League Service, 'Exhibition of Practical Arts', *XXI Gallery*, London (November-December 1919)

Badovici 1925: J. Badovici, *L'Architecture Vivante, Automne et Hiver*, Paris 1925

Baljeu 1968: J. Baljeu, 'De vierde dimensie', in: J. Leering et al., *Theo van Doesburg 1883–1931*, Eindhoven/The Hague/Basel 1968, pp. 9-15

Baljeu 1974: J. Baljeu, *Theo van Doesburg*, London 1974

Banham 1960: R. Banham, *Theory and Design in the First Machine Age*, London 1960, ed. 1988

Barbieri et al. 1983: S.U. Barbieri et al., *Theo Van Doesburg. Grondbegrippen van de nieuwe beeldende kunst*, Nijmegen 1983

Benevolo 1960: L. Benevolo, *Storia dell'architettura moderna*, Bari 1960, English trans. *Modern Architecture*, parts I and II, London 1971

Benton 2006: T. Benton, *The Modernist Home*, London 2006

Bergdoll and Christensen 2008: B. Bergdoll and P. Christensen, *Home Delivery. Fabricating the Modern Dwelling*, New York 2008

Van Bergeijk 2007: H. van Bergeijk, *Jan Wils, De Stijl en verder*, Rotterdam 2007

Berlage 1922: H.P. Berlage, 'Beschouwingen over stijl', in: *Studies over bouwkunst, stijl en samenleving*, 2nd impression, Rotterdam 1922

Bless 1982: F. Bless, *Rietveld 1888–1964. Een biografie*, Amsterdam 1982

Blotkamp 1982: C. Blotkamp (ed.), *De Stijl 1917–1922. The Formative Years*, Cambridge (Mass.)/London 1982 (ed. 1990)

Blotkamp 1984: C. Blotkamp, 'Rietveld en De Stijl', in: B. Mulder and G.J. de Rook (eds.), *Rietveld-Schröderhuis*, Utrecht 1984, pp. 5-14

Blotkamp 1987: C. Blotkamp, 'Mondriaan – Architectuur', in: C. Blotkamp, *Mondriaan in detail*, Utrecht/Antwerp 1987, pp. 9-101

Bock 1993: M. Bock, 'Inleiding', in: V. van Rossem, *Het Algemeen Uitbreidingsplan van Amsterdam. Geschiedenis en ontwerp*, Rotterdam 1993

Bock 1996: M. Bock, 'Cornelis van Eesteren', in: C. Blotkamp (ed.), *De vervolgjaren van De Stijl 1922–1932*, Amsterdam/Antwerp, pp. 241-295

Bock 2001: M. Bock, 'Architectonische ontwerpen, 1922–1924', in: M. Bock, V. van Rossem and K. Somer, *Bouwkunst, stijl, stedenbouw. Van Eesteren en de avant-garde*, Rotterdam/ The Hague 2001, pp. 135-208

Bock, Van Rossem and Somer 2001: M. Bock, V. van Rossem and K. Somer, *Bouwkunst, stijl, stedenbouw. Van Eesteren en de avant-garde*, Rotterdam/The Hague 2001

Boekraad 1983a: C. Boekraad (ed.), *Theo van Doesburg. Naar een beeldende architectuur*, Nijmegen 1983

Boekraad 1983b: C. Boekraad, 'Stijl en anti-stijl/Style and anti-Style', in: C. Boekraad (ed.), *Het Nieuwe Bouwen. De Stijl. De Nieuwe Beelding in de architectuur. Neo Plasticism in Architecture*, The Hague/Delft 1983, pp. 50-100

Boekraad 1986: C. Boekraad (ed.) Theo van Doesburg. De Stijl en de Europese architectuur. De architectuuropstellen in Het Bouwbedrijf, 1924-1931, Nijmegen 1986, translation: '*Theo van Doesburg. On European Architecture. Complete Essays from Het Bouwbedrijf 1924–1931*, Basel/Berlin/Boston 1990

Bois 1983: Y.-A. Bois, 'De Stijl in Parijs/ De Stijl in Paris', in: C. Boekraad (ed.), *Het Nieuwe Bouwen. De Stijl. De Nieuwe Beelding in de architectuur. Neo Plasticism in Architecture*, The Hague/Delft 1983, pp. 101-127

Bois 1985: Y.-A. Bois, 'L'idee De Stijl', in: Y.-A. Bois and B. Reichlin et al., *De Stijl et l'architecture en France*, Paris 1985, pp. 11-16

Bois 1987: Y.-A. Bois, 'Mondrian and the Theory of Architecture', *Assemblage* 2 (1987) 4, pp. 103-130

Bois et al. 1985: Y.-A. Bois et al., *De Stijl et l'architecture en France*, Paris 1985

Van Bommel 2009: A.J. van Bommel, 'Het Rietveld paviljoen bij het Kröller-Müller Museum. Over de voorgenomen reconstructie van 2010', *Praktijkreeks Cultureel Erfgoed* 9 (December 2009) no. 24

Bos 1937: M.C. Bos, 'Experimental Study of Productive Collaboration', *Acta Psychologica* III 1937 (1938) 3, pp. 315-426

Van den Broek et al. 1951: J.H. van den Broek et al., *De Stijl. Cat. 81, Stedelijk Museum Amsterdam*, Amsterdam 1951

Broekhuizen 2000: D. Broekhuizen, *De Stijl toen – J.J.P. Oud nu. De bijdrage van J.J.P. Oud aan herdenken, herstellen en bouwen in Nederland (1938–1963)*, Rotterdam 2000

Broekhuizen 2010: D. Broekhuizen (ed.) 2010: *Robert van 't Hoff. Architect of a New Society*, Rotterdam 2010

Brown 1958: T.M. Brown, *The Work of G. Rietveld. Architect*, Cambridge, Mass. 1958

Brown 1965: T.M. Brown, 'Rietveld's Egocentric Vision', *The Society of Architectural Historians Journal* 24 (1965) 4, pp. 292-296

Bruijn, Ten Heuvelhof and In 't Veld 2010: H. Bruijn, E. ten Heuvelhof and R. In 't Veld, *Process Management. Why Project Management Fails in Complex Decision Making Processes*, New York 2010

Dannenmann 2014: M. Dannenmann, 'Mies 1:1 2013', in: C. Lange et al., *Mies 1:1. Ludwig Mies van der Rohe. The Golf Club Project/ Das Golfclub Projekt*, Cologne 2014, pp. 84-100

Dettingmeijer 2010: R. Dettingmeijer 2010: 'Rietveld and the Writing of Architecture History', in: R. Dettingmeijer, M.-T. van Thoor, I. van Zijl (eds.), *Rietveld's Universe*, Rotterdam, pp. 20-35

Van Doesburg 1918: [T. van Doesburg], 'Aanteekeningen over monumentale kunst', *De Stijl* II (November 1918) 1, pp. 10-12, appendix 1

Van Doesburg 1920: T. van Doesburg, 'L'Art Monumental', *Lumière* (April 1920); also in: *Terramar* 2 (June 1920) 23/24, 3-4; *Bleu* (July 1920), p. 2

Van Doesburg 1923a: T. van Doesburg, 'Zur Elementaren Gestaltung', *G. Material zur elementaren Gestaltung* 1 (June 1923)

Van Doesburg 1923b: T. van Doesburg, 'Voorwaarden tot een nieuwe architectuur', *Architectura, weekblad van het genootschap Architectura et Amicitia* 27 (11 August 1923) 27, pp. 163-165

Van Doesburg 1924a: T. van Doesburg, 'Tot een beeldende architectuur, *De Stijl* VI (1924) 6/7, pp. 78-83

Van Doesburg, 1924b: T. van Doesburg, 'De nieuwe architectuur', *Bouwkundig Weekblad* 45 (17 May 1924) 20, pp. 200-204

Van Doesburg 1925a: T. van Doesburg, *Grundbegriffe der neuen gestaltenden Kunst (Neue Bauhausbücher 6)*, Munich 1925 (Mainz/Berlin 1966)

Van Doesburg 1925b: T. van Doesburg, 'L'Evolution de l'architecture Moderne en Hollande', *L'Architecture Vivante* III (autumn/winter 1925) 9, pp. 14-20

Van Doesburg and Van Eesteren 1924: Van Doesburg and Van Eesteren 1924: T. van Doesburg and C. van Eesteren, 'Vers une construction collective' and '-□+=R4', *De Stijl* 6 (1924) 6/7, pp. 89-91

Van Doesburg et al. 1918: T. van Doesburg et al., 'Manifest 1 van De Stijl', *De Stijl* II (1918) 1, pp. 2-3

Doig 1986: A. Doig, *Theo van Doesburg. Painting into Architecture, Theory into Practice*, Cambridge/New York 1986

Van Duijn and Verheul 2015: D. van Duijn and W.J. Verheul, 'De staat als twaalfde man. Zijn overheidsinvesteringen in een stadion van waarde voor de stad?', *Bestuurskunde* 24 (2015) 4, pp. 70-81

Dumont d'Ayot and Benton 2013: C. Dumont d'Ayot and T. Benton, *Le Corbusier's Pavilion for Zurich. Model and Prototype of an Ideal Exhibition Space*, Zurich 2013

Edwards 2000: P. Edwards, 'Introduction', in: P. Edwards (ed.), *Blast. Vorticism 1914–1918*, Aldershot 2000

Eekhout 2000: M. Eekhout, *Over de 'bouwbaarheid' van het Maison d'Artiste. Overwegingen omtrent technische uitvoerbaarheid*, Amsterdam 2000

Eekhout 2015: M. Eekhout, *Emeritaatsrede. Technologisch ontwerpen in spagaat tussen innovaties en wetenschap*, Delft, 20 March 2015

Van Eesteren 1931: C. van Eesteren, 'C. van Eesteren and Theo van Doesburg. Ontwerp voor een vrijstaand woonhuis (1922), in: C. van der Sluys, *Onze woning en haar inrichting*, Amsterdam 1931, pp. 37-38

Engel 2009: H. Engel, 'Theo van Doesburg and the Destruction of Architectural Theory', in: G. Fabre and D. Wintgens Hötte (eds.), *Constructing a New World. Van Doesburg and the International Avant-Garde*, London/Leiden 2009, pp. 36-45

Ex 1996: S. Ex, 'De blik naar het oosten. De Stijl in Duitsland en Oost-Europa', in: C. Blotkamp (ed.), *De vervolgjaren van De Stijl, 1922–1932*, Amsterdam/Antwerp 1996, pp. 67-112

Ex 2000: S. Ex, *Theo van Doesburg en het Bauhaus. De invloed van De Stijl in Duitsland en Midden-Europa*, Utrecht 2000

Ex and Hoek 1985: S. Ex and E. Hoek, *Vilmos Huszár. Schilder en ontwerper, 1884–1960*, Utrecht 1985

Fabre 2016: G.C. Fabre (ed.), *Theo van Doesburg. Een nieuwe kijk op leven, kunst en technologie*, Brussels (Bozar Paleis voor Schone Kunsten) 2016

Fanelli 1985: G. Fanelli, *Stijl-Architektur. Die niederländische Beitrag zur frühen Moderne*, Stuttgart 1985

Florida 2008: R. Florida, *Who's your city? How the creative economy is making where to live the most important decision of your life*, Philadelphia 2008

Friedel 2011: H. Friedel, 'Mondrian und De Stijl/Mondrian and De Stijl', in: H. Friedel et al., *Mondrian. De Stijl*, Ostfildern 2011, pp. 6-9

Friedman 1982: M. Friedman (ed.) 1982: *De Stijl 1917–1931. Visions of Utopia*, Oxford 1982

Galison, Holton and Schweber 2008: P.L. Galison, G. Holton and S.S. Schweber, *Einstein for the 21st Century. His Legacy in Science, Art and Modern Culture*, Princeton 2008

Van Gameren et al. 2013: D. van Gameren et al., *Woningbouw-tentoonstellingen/Housing Exhibitions. Delft Architectural Studies on Housing*, Rotterdam 2013

Gasten 1978: A. Gasten, 'Pseudo-mathematica en Beeldende kunst', in: C. Blotkamp et al., *Kunstenaren der idee. Symbolistische tendenzen in Nederland, ca. 1880–1930*, The Hague 1978, pp. 59-66

Gehl 2010: J. Gehl, *Cities for people*, Washington 2010
Giedion 1941: S. Giedion, *Space, Time and Architecture. The Growth of a New Tradition*, Cambridge, Mass. 1941
Goddijn 2000: A. Goddijn, 'Recreatieve wiskunde. Ars et Mathesis', *Nieuwsbrief nieuw archive voor wiskunde* (September 2000) 3, pp. 339-341
Gonzalez and Guadiana 2013: E.R. Gonzalez and L. Guadiana, 'Culture-Led Downtown Regeneration or Creative Gentrification?', in: M.E. Leary and J. McCarthy, *The Routledge Companian to Urban Regeneration*, London 2013, pp. 536-547
Groenendijk 2003: P. Groenendijk, 'Arcam-gebouw Amsterdam, René van Zuuk', *Bouw* no. 11, November 2003, pp. 22-25
Guigon 2006: E. Guigon et al., *De Aubette of de kleur in de architectuur*, Rotterdam 2006
Hanssen 2015: L. Hanssen, *De schepping van een aards paradijs. Piet Mondriaan 1919–1933*, Amsterdam 2015
Healey 2010: P. Healey, *Making Better Places. The Planning Project in the Twenty-First Century*, Basingstoke 2010
Hemel 1994: Z. Hemel, *Het landschap en de IJsselmeerpolders. Planning, inrichting en vormgeving*, Rotterdam 1994
Henket et al. 2004: H.-J. Henket et al., *Het Van Doesburghuis. Ontmoetingen in Meudon/La Maison Van Doesburg. Rencontres à Meudon*, Bussum 2004
Hitchcock Jr. 1929: H.-R. Hitchcock Jr., *Modern Architecture. Romanticism and Reintegration*, New York 1929 (1993)
Hitchcock 1958: H.-R. Hitchcock, *Architecture. Nineteenth and Twentieth Centuries*, New Haven/London 1985
Hoek 2000: E. Hoek (ed.), *Theo van Doesburg Oeuvre Catalogue*, Utrecht/Otterlo 2000
Hoekema 2014: S. Hoekema, *De Stijl (1956) als reactie op De Stijl (1951). Een onderzoek naar het proefschrift van Hans Jaffé*, MA thesis general cultural sciences, University of Amsterdam, October 2014
Hospers 2013: G.J. Hospers, *Geografie en gevoel. Wat plekken met ons doen*, Assen 2013
Idsinga and Schilt 1987: T. Idsinga and J. Schilt, *Architect W. van Tijen 1894–1974. 'Ik ben een rationalist, maar er is meer op de wereld...'*., The Hague s.a. [1987]
Jaeggi 2009: A. Jaeggi (ed.), *Bauhaus a Conceptual Model*, Berlin/Ostfildern 2009
Jaffé 1956: H.L.C. Jaffé, *De Stijl 1917–1931. The Dutch Contribution to Modern Art*, Amsterdam 1956 (1986)
Jaffé 1983: H.L.C. Jaffé, *Theo van Doesburg*, [Amsterdam] 1983
Janssen and White 2011: H. Janssen and M. White, *Het verhaal van De Stijl. Van Mondriaan tot Van Doesburg*, Antwerp/The Hague (Gemeente Museum) 2011
Janssen 2012: H. Janssen, 'De eerste gedaantes van Victory Boogie Woogie', in: M. van Bommel, H. Janssen and R. Spronk (eds.), *Victory Boogie Woogie uitgepakt. Geschiedenis van Mondriaans meesterwerk*, Amsterdam 2012, pp. 179-202
John-Steiner 2000: V. John-Steiner, *Creative Collaboration*, New York 2000
John-Steiner 2003: V. John-Steiner, 'Thinking Together: Connections and Separations in Joint Endeavors', *Contemporary Psychology. APA Review of Books* 48 (2003) 3, pp. 347-349
Johnson and Barr jr. 1952: P.C. Johnson and A.H. Barr jr., *De Stijl 1917–1928. The Museum of Modern Art Bulletin* XX (1952–1953) 2
De Jong 2015: C.W. de Jong (ed.), *De ateliers van Piet Mondriaan, Amsterdam, Laren, Parijs, London, New York,* Amsterdam 2015
De Jonge 2007: W. de Jonge, 'Het Philips-paviljoen: van 1958 naar 2008? Haalbaarheidsonderzoek voor reconstructie', in: Stichting Alice, *Make it New: Le poème électronique. Onderzoek voor de reconstructie van het Philips-paviljoen uit 1958 in Eindhoven*, Eindhoven 2007, pp. 11-19

De Jonge 2010: W. de Jonge, 'Bouwhistorisch onderzoek naar gebouwen van de moderne beweging', 'Onderzoek en restauratieplan' en 'Restauratieconcept', in: P. Meurs and M.-Th. van Thoor (eds.), *Sanatorium Zonnestraal, geschiedenis en restauratie van een modern monument/Zonnestraal Sanatorium, The History and Restoration of a Modern Monument*, Rotterdam/Delft, pp. 101-110, 160-169 and 179-185

Junghanns 1994: K. Junghanns, *Das Haus für Alle. Zur Geschichte der Vorfertigung in Deutschland*, Berlin 1994

Kaplan 1996: W. Kaplan, *Charles Rennie Mackintosh*, Glasgow (etc.) 1996

Klingmann 2007: A. Klingmann, *Brandscapes. Architecture in the experience economy*, Cambridge 2007

Koolhaas et al. 2014: R. Koolhaas et al., *Fundamentals catalogue. 14th international architecture exhibition*, Venice 2014

Van Kooten and Bloemheuvel 2007: T. van Kooten and M. Bloemheuvel, *Sculpture Garden Kröller-Müller Museum*, Rotterdam/Otterlo 2007

Koppenjan 2004: E. H. Klijn and J. Koppenjan, *Managing Uncertenties in Networks*, London 2004

Kossmann and De Jong 2010: H. Kossmann and M. de Jong (eds.), *Engaging Spaces. Exhibition Design Explored by Kossmann. dejong*, Amsterdam 2001

Kuipers 1984: M. Kuipers, 'Inleiding/Introduction', in: V. Veldhuijzen van Zanten and T. Mees, *Maison d'Artiste. Bouwplaat/Scale model kit 1:100*, Gouda/Amsterdam 1984

Kuipers 2006: M. Kuipers, 'Op zoek naar het verloren feest: vragen over authenticiteit, beeld en herinnering', in: E. Guigon et al., *De Aubette of de kleur in de architectuur*, Rotterdam 2006, pp. 180-189

Kuper 1982: M. Kuper, 'Gerrit Rietveld', in: C. Blotkamp (ed.), *De Stijl 1917–1922. The Formative Years*, Cambridge (Mass.)/London 1982 (ed. 1990), pp. 259-277

Kuper and Van Zijl 1992: M. Kuper and I. van Zijl, *Gerrit Th. Rietveld 1888–1964.The complete works*, Utrecht 1992

Kuper 2010: 'Rietveld and De Stijl', in: R. Dettingmeijer, M.-T. van Thoor and I. van Zijl (ed.), *Rietveld's Universe*, Rotterdam 2010, pp. 194-211

Kuper 2011: M. Kuper, *De stoel van Rietveld/Rietveld's Chair*, Rotterdam 2011

Lampugnani and Schneider 1992: V.M. Lampugnani and R. Schneider (eds.), *Moderne Architektur in Deutschland 1900 bis 1950. Reform und Tradition*, Stuttgart 1992

Lange 2014a: C. Lange (ed.), *Mies 1:1. Ludwig Mies van der Rohe. The Golf Club Project/Das Golfclub Projekt*, Cologne 2014

Lange 2014b: C. Lange 2014: 'Mies 1:1. The Golf club project/ Mies 1:1 Das Golfclub Projekt', in: C. Lange et al., *Mies 1:1. Ludwig Mies van der Rohe. The Golf Club Project/ Das Golfclub Projekt*, Cologne 2014, pp. 62-82

Langmead 1999: D. Langmead, *J.J.P.Oud and the International Style. A Bio-Bibliography*, Westport CT/London 1999

Le Coultre 2015: M.F. Le Coultre, *De hut van Mondriaan. Laren-Blaricum 1914–1919*, Laren/Naarden 2015

Leering 1968: J. Leering, 'De architectuur en Van Doesburg', in: J. Leering et al., *Theo van Doesburg 1883–1931*, Eindhoven/ The Hague/Basel 1968, pp. 19-25

Lehning 2001: P. Lehning, *De mondialisering van het lokale. Afscheidsrede*, Rotterdam Erasmus University, Rotterdam 2001

Levine 2008: N. Levine, 'Building the Unbuilt: Authenticity and the Archive', *Journal of the Society of Architectural Historians* 67 (2008) 1, pp. 14-17

Lewis 1919: W. Lewis, *The Caliph's Design. Architects! Where is Your Vortex?*, London 1919

Lodder 2006: C. Lodder, 'Searching for Utopia', in: C. Wilk (ed.), *Modernism 1914–1939. Designing a New World*, London 2006, pp. 23-69

Van Loghem 1932: J.B. van Loghem, U. Barbieri (intro.), *Ir. J.B. van Loghem. Bouwen, bauen, bâtir, building – Holland. Een dokumentatie van de hoogtepunten van de moderne architektuur in Nederland*, Amsterdam 1932 (Nijmegen 1980)

Mallgrave and Robinson 2004: H.F. Mallgrave and M. Robinson (eds.), *Style in the Technical and Tectonic Arts*, Los Angeles 2004

Manacorda and White 2014: F. Manacorda and M. White (eds.), *Mondrian and His Studios. Colour in Space*, London 2014

Martin and Smals 2001: M. Martin and J. Smals, *Wall House #2 John Hejduk*, Groningen 2001

De Meijer et al. 1918: J. de Meijer et al., 'Jury-rapport over de ingekomen antwoorden op de prijsvraag voor den aanleg van een centraal-punt in het IJ-bosch', *Bouwkundig Weekblad* 39 (25 May 1918) 21, pp. 126-128

Mesnil 1923: J. Mesnil, 'Les expositions', *L'Humanité*, 28 October 1923

Meurs 1992: P. Meurs, 'Nederland als utopie, Holland Village in Japan', *de Architect* no. 7/8, 1992, pp. 22-33

Meurs 2008: P. Meurs, 'Restoration without dogma, guidelines, from general to specific', in: P. Meurs, *Building in the Stubborn City*, Delft 2008, pp. 53-89

Meurs 2016: P. Meurs, *Heritage-Based Design*, Delft 2016

Mondrian 1919: P. Mondrian, 'Natuurlijke en abstracte realiteit', *De Stijl* 2 (October 1919) 12, pp. 133-137, transl. 'Natural Reality and Abstract Reality. A Trialogue, in: H. Holtzman and M.S. James (eds.), *The New Art – The New Life. The Collected Writings of Piet Mondrian*, New York 1993, pp. 82-123

Mondrian 1927: P. Mondrian, 'Neo-plasticisme: De Woning – De Straat – De Stad', *i10* 1 (1927) 1, pp. 12-18; transl. 'Home - Street – City', in: H. Holtzman, M.S. James (ed.), *The New Art – The New Life. The Collected Writings of Piet Mondrian*, New York 1993, pp. 205-212

Van Moorsel 2000: W. van Moorsel, *Nelly van Doesburg 1899–1975. 'De doorsnee is mij niet genoeg'*, Nijmegen 2000

Mulder 2011: B. Mulder, 'Het reconstrueren van gebouwd erfgoed', in: S. Stroux et al., *Recomomo. Hoe echt is namaak, hoe dierbaar het origineel?'*, Docomomo-nl (May 2011) 2, pp. 46-51

Münch 2003: A. Münch, *De Stijl, das geometrische Ornament und die monumentale Gestaltung*, Bern 2003

Migayrou 2010: F. Migayrou (ed.), *De Stijl 1917–1931*, Paris 2010

Nelissen 2003: N.J.M. Nelissen, *Strijd om architectuur in Europa. Een kleine mars door de geschiedenis*, Maastricht/Nijmegen 2003

Noell 2011: M. Noell, *Im Laboratorium der Moderne. Das Atelierwohnhaus von Theo van Doesburg in Meudon – Architektur zwischen Abstraktion und Rhetorik*, Zurich 2011

Ottevanger 2008: A. Ottevanger, '*De Stijl overal absolute leiding.' De briefwisseling tussen Theo van Doesburg en Anthony Kok*, Bussum 2008

Oud 1913: J.J.P. Oud, 'Onze eigen bouwstijl', *Bouwkundig Weekblad* 33 (10 May 1913) 19, p. 223

Oud 1919: J.J.P. Oud, 'Oriëntatie', *De Stijl* 3 (December 1919) 2, pp. 13-15

Oud 1921: J.J.P. Oud, 'Over de toekomstige bouwkunst en hare architectonische mogelijkheden', *Bouwkundig Weekblad* 42 (11 June 1921) 24, pp. 147-160

Overmeiere and Patijn 1990: K. Overmeiere and W. Patijn, 'Het begin van een restauratie. Verslag van de reconstructie van een woonblok', in: S. Cusveller (ed.), *De Kiefhoek. Een woonwijk in Rotterdam*, Laren 1990, pp. 93-111

Overy 1991: P. Overy, *De Stijl. Art, Architecture, Design*, London 1991 (2000)

Ozinga 1961: M.D. Ozinga, *Proeve van een monumentenlijst voor Suriname*, May 1961

Padovan 1981: R. Padovan, 'The pavilion and the court. Cultural and spatial problems of De Stijl architecture', *The Architectural Review* CLXX (December 1981) 1018, pp. 359-368

Polano 1982: S. Polano 1982: 'De Stijl/Architecture = Nieuwe Beelding', in: M. Friedman (ed.), 1982: *De Stijl 1917–1931. Visions of Utopia*, Oxford 1982, pp. 87-97

Postma and Boekraad et al. 1995: F. Postma and C. Boekraad et al., *26 Rue du Départ. Mondriaans atelier in Parijs 1921–1936*, Berlin 1995

Rambosson 1923: Y. Rambosson, 'Les architectes du groupe De Styl', *L'Amour de l'Art*, (December 1923) 12

Ritzer 1993: G. Ritzer, *The McDonaldization of Society*, London 1993

Ritzer 2007: G. Ritzer, 'The Globalization of Nothing', *SAIS Review* 23 (2007) 2

Roodenburg-Schadd 2004: C. Roodenburg-Schadd, *Expressie en ordening. Het verzamelbeleid van Willem Sandberg voor het Stedelijk Museum 1945–1962*, Amsterdam/Rotterdam 2004

Van Rossem 1993: V. van Rossem, *Het Algemeen Uitbreidingsplan van Amsterdam. Geschiedenis en ontwerp*, Rotterdam 1993

Schlösser et al. 1980: M. Schlösser et al., *Arbeitsrat für Kunst. Berlin 1918–1921*, Berlin 1980

Schumacher 2007: R.W.G. Schumacher, *Museumjournaal als forum van een nieuw kunstbegrip*, Utrecht 2007

Shaw 1932: M.E. Shaw, 'A Comparison of Individuals and Small Groups in the Rational Solution of Complex Problems', *American Journal of Psychology* 44 (1932), pp. 491-505

Sirag 1941: M. Sirag, *Bouwmaterialen Polytechnische Bibliotheek*, no. 57, 1941 (7th impression)

Sklair 2006: L. Sklair, 'Iconic Architecture and Capitalist Globalization', *City: analysis of urban trends, culture, theory, policy, action*, 10 (2006) 1

Somer 2007: K. Somer, *The Functional City. The CIAM and Cornelis van Eesteren, 1928–1960*, Rotterdam/The Hague 2007

Spierings 2006: B.H.A. Spierings, *Cities, Consumption and Competition. The Image of Consumerism and the Making of City Centres*, Nijmegen 2006

Steenhuis and Meurs 2012: M. Steenhuis and P. Meurs, *Herbestemming in Nederland*, Rotterdam 2012

Van Straaten et al. 1983: E. van Straaten et al., *Theo van Doesburg 1883–1931. Een documentaire op basis van materiaal uit de schenking Van Moorsel*, The Hague 1983

Van Straaten 1988: E. van Straaten: *Theo van Doesburg. Painter and Architect*, The Hague 1988

Van Straaten 1996: E. van Straaten, 'Theo van Doesburg', in: C. Blotkamp (ed.), *De vervolgjaren van De Stijl 1922–1932*, Amsterdam/Antwerp 1996, pp. 15-66

Stroux and Quist 2011: S. Stroux and W. Quist, 'Recomomo. Hoe echt is namaak, hoe dierbaar het origineel?', in: S. Stroux et al., *Recomomo. Hoe echt is namaak, hoe dierbaar het origineel?*, Docomomo-nl (May 2011) 2, pp. 4-7

Surowiecki 2004: J. Surowiecki, *The Wisdom of Crowds*, New York 2004

Suttorp 1994: M. Suttorp, 'Mondriaans atelier, "aardsch paradijs"', *kM, Mondriaan special* 12 (winter 1994), pp. 44-47

Taverne and Broekhuizen 1995: E. Taverne and D. Broekhuizen, *Het Shell-gebouw van J.J.P. Oud. Ontwerp en receptie/ J.J.P. Oud's Shell Building. Design and Reception*, Rotterdam 1995

Taverne and Broekhuizen 1996: E. Taverne and D. Broekhuizen, 'De dissidente architecten: J.J.P. Oud, Jan Wils and Robert van 't Hoff', in: C. Blotkamp (ed.), *De vervolgjaren van De Stijl 1922–1932*, Amsterdam/Antwerp 1996, pp. 361-396

Temminck Groll et al. 1973: C.L. Temminck Groll et al., *De architektuur van Suriname, 1667–1930*, Zutphen 1973

Tempel, Janssen and Van der Tholen 2011: B. Tempel, H. Janssen and S. van der Tholen, *Mondriaan en De Stijl. Een definitieve plek in Nederland/ A Permanent Home in The Netherlands*, The Hague 2011

Termeer 2007: K. Termeer, *Vitale verschillen. Over leiderschap en maatschappelijke innovatie*, Wageningen 2007

Thorissen 1995: E. Thorissen, *De tentoonstelling 'Les architectes du groupe De Stijl' in galerie L'Effort Moderne te Parijs 15 oktober-15 november 1923 in een bredere context geplaatst*, unpublished thesis, University of Nijmegen 1995
Troy 1979: N.J. Troy, *De Stijl's Collaborative Ideal: the Colored Abstract Environment, 1916–1926*, New Haven (Ann Arbor 1986)
Troy 1982: N.J. Troy 1982: 'The Abstract Environment of De Stijl', in: M. Friedman (ed.), 1982: *De Stijl 1917–1931. Visions of Utopia*, Oxford, pp. 165-189
Troy 1983: N.J. Troy, *The De Stijl Environment*, Cambridge, Mass./ London 1983
Troy 2014: N.J. Troy, *The Afterlife of Piet Mondrian*, Chicago 2014
Varkki George 1997: R. Varkki George, 'A Procedural Explanation for Contemporary Design', *Journal of Urban Design* 2 (1997) 2, pp. 143-161
Veissière 1923: G. Veissière, 'Les architectes du groupe De Stijl', *L'Architecture*, 36 (1923) 22
Veldhuijzen van Zanten 2006: V. Veldhuijzen van Zanten, *Maison d'Artiste 2000* (design notes), Rotterdam 2006
Veldhuijzen van Zanten 2011: V. Veldhuijzen van Zanten, 'De realisatie van het Maison d'Artiste op schaal 1:1', in: S. Stroux et al., *Recomomo. Hoe echt is namaak, hoe dierbaar het origineel?*, Docomomo-nl (May 2011) 2, pp. 60-63
Verheul 2012: W.J. Verheul, *Stedelijke iconen. Het ontstaan van beeldbepalende projecten tussen betoog en beton*, The Hague 2012
Verheul 2013a: W.J. Verheul, 'Iconische projecten maken furore, maar zijn ze ook verankerd?', *de Architect* February 2013
Verheul, 2013b: W.J. Verheul, 'Op zoek naar de heilige graal van katalysatorprojecten in stadsontwikkeling', *Real Estate Research Quarterly* 12 (December 2013) 4, pp. 51-58
Verheul and Daamen 2014: W.J. Verheul and T.A. Daamen, 'Stedelijke ontwikkeling als emergente adaptieve strategie', *Bestuurswetenschappen* 68 (2014) 3, pp. 68-88
Vink 1990: H.J. Vink, 'Ruimte en tijd in de geschriften van Severini, Vantongerloo, Mondriaan en Van Doesburg', *Jong Holland*, 6 (1990) 2, pp. 2-13, and 6 (1990) 3, pp. 2-19
Warncke 1998: C.-P. Warncke, *De Stijl 1917–1931*, Cologne 1998
Watkin 1986: D. Watkin, *De westerse architectuur. Een geschiedenis*, Nijmegen 1986 (2000)
Wever 2015: P. Wever, *Inside Le Corbusier's Philips Pavilion. A Multimedial Space at the 1958 Brussels World's Fair*, Rotterdam 2015
White 2003: M. White, *De Stijl and Dutch Modernism*, Manchester 2003
White 2011: M. White, 'De Stijl: An Art for the People?/ De Stijl: Eine Kunst fürs Volk?', in: H. Friedel et al., *Mondrian. De Stijl*, Ostfildern 2011, pp. 47-62
Wieczorek 2010: M. Wieczorek, 'Le paradigme De Stijl', in: F. Migayrou (ed.), *De Stijl 1917–1931*, Paris (Centre Georges Pompidou) 2010, pp. 64-75
Wigley 1995: M. Wigley, *White Walls, Designer Dresses. The Fashioning of Modern Architecture*, Cambridge, Mass./London 1995
Wils 1918: J. Wils, 'Symmetrie en kultuur', *De Stijl*, 1 (October 1918) 12, pp. 137-139
Van der Wolk 1992: J. van der Wolk (ed.), *De Kröllers en hun architecten*, Otterlo 1992
Van der Woud 2015: A. van der Woud, *De nieuwe mens. De culturele revolutie in Nederland rond 1900*, Amsterdam 2015
Zevi 1953: B. Zevi, *Poetica dell'architettura neoplastica*, Milan 1953
Zevi 1969: B. Zevi, 'Theo van Doesburg – morgen', *Museumjournaal* 14 (1969) 1, pp. 59-63
Van Zijl and Mulder 2009: I. van Zijl and B. Mulder, *Het Rietveld Schröderhuis*, Utrecht 2009
Zukin 2010: S. Zukin, *The Naked City. Life and Death of Urban Authentic Places*, Oxford 2010

# Index

## Names

**Places**

# Archives

Abbreviations in notes refer to the following archives

Amsterdam, Stedelijk Museum (SMA)
– file: exhibition 'De Stijl, 1951', and photo collection
The Hague, RKD – Netherlands Institute for Art History
– archive Theo and Nelly van Doesburg (VDA)
Eindhoven, Van Abbemuseum (VA)
– file: exhibition 'Theo van Doesburg', 1968
Paris, Fondation Custodia (FC)
– Collection Frits Lugt
Paris, Centre Pompidou (CP)
– archive Rosenberg, Bibliothèque Kandinsky
Rotterdam, Het Nieuwe Instituut (previously Netherlands Architecture Insitute) HNI
– archive W.F. van Bodegraven, BODE
– archive J.H. van den Broek, BROZ
– archive T. van Doesburg, DOES
– archive C. van Eesteren, EEST
– archive J. Leering, LEER
– archive J.J.P. Oud, correspondence files, OUDJ
– archive G.T. Rietveld, RIET
– archive J. Wils, WILS
Rotterdam, private archive Stichting Realisatie Maison d'Artiste (SRMA)
Utrecht, Centraal Museum, Rietveld-Schröder Archive, CMU, RSA
– file: exhibition 'De Stijl 1917–1928', and photo collection RS

# Illustration credits

Archives Van Abbemuseum, Eindhoven / photo Van den Bichelaer, Geldrop 16
Dolf Broekhuizen 20, 55, 57, 120
Centraal Museum, Utrecht / photo Ernst Moritz 14
Collection Van Abbemuseum, Eindhoven / photo Peter Cox, Eindhoven 50
© Martien Coppens / Nederlands Fotomuseum, Rotterdam 10, 17
Fondation Custodia, Collection Frits Lugt, Paris 26, 27, 28
Findhorn 119
Gemeentemuseum Den Haag 58
Rob 't Hart 107
Het Nieuwe Instituut, Rotterdam / archive Theo van Doesburg (DOES) 43, 44, 48, 60, 61, 62, 68, 69, 70, 71, 72, 73, 75, 76, 77, 78, 79, 80, 81, 102, 103
Het Nieuwe Instituut, Rotterdam / archive Cornelis van Eesteren (EEST), loan Van Eesteren-
Fluck & Van Lohuizen Stichting (EFL Stichting) 1, 2, 3, 4, 18, 29, 30, 31, 32, 33, 34, 35, 36, 37, 39, 49, 51, 52, 53, 63, 64, 65, 66, 67, 74, 82, 85, 86, 87, 88, 89, 90, 91
Het Nieuwe Instituut, Rotterdam / archive models (MAQV) 84
Het Nieuwe Instituut, Rotterdam / archive Jan Wils (WILS) 41, 42
House for an Art Lover 111
Juurlink [+] Geluk Stedenbouw en Landschap 110
Fas Keuzenkamp 59
Maarten Kloos 97
Korteknie Stuhlmacher Architecten 21
Kröller-Müller Museum, Otterlo 121
Jannes Linders 112, 113, 114
Cary Markerink 19
Paul Meurs 115
DIGITAL IMAGE © (August 2016) Museum of Modern Art, New York/ Scala, Florence 83
Norbert van Onna 108
Österreichische Nationalbibliothek (ONB)/Vienna Picture Archive H 1136/1 / photo Albert Hilscher 13
Penta Architecten 106
Full-scale reconstruction: Frans Postma, Delft; Collection: STAM / photo Fas Keuzenkamp 15
Christian Richters 105, 118
Rietveld Schröder archive / Centraal Museum, Utrecht 54
RKD – Netherlands Institute for Art History, The Hague / archive Theo and Nelly van Doesburg 5, 8, 22, 25, 40, 45, 100, 101
RKD – Netherlands Institute for Art History, The Hague / archive Piet Mondriaan 11
Robbrecht en Daem architecten / photo Thomas Hick 116, 117
Stichting Realisatie Maison d'Artiste 92 (Luuk de Boer), 93, 94, 95, 96
Thijs Wolzak 104
Erwin Zijlstra 109

# About the authors

**Ole Bouman** is a cultural and architectural historian. From 2006 to 2012 he was director of the Netherlands Architecture Institute in Rotterdam. Since 2016 he has been director of Design Society, which opens in Shenzhen, China, in 2017.

**Dr. Dolf Broekhuizen** is an architectural historian and works as a freelance consultant, researcher and author on the subject of twentieth-century cultural heritage.

**Professor Dr. Paul Meurs** is Professor of Heritage and Cultural Value at Delft Technical University and also partner in SteenhuisMeurs, a cultural history consultancy in Paterswolde and Rotterdam.

**Dr. Alied Ottevanger** is curator of 20th-century printing and drawing at the Rijksmuseum Amsterdam.

**Dr. Kees Somer** is an architecture historian with the Ministry of Education, Cultural Affairs and Science where he works in the Cultural Heritage Agency.

**Dr. Wouter Jan Verheul** is a public administration expert employed in the Architecture Faculty's Department of Management in the Built Environment at TU Delft and a freelance consultant in Rotterdam.

**Professor Michael White** teaches in the History of Art Department at the University of York.

# Acknowledgements

*Maison d'Artiste. Unfinished De Stijl Icon* is published to mark the fact that in 2017 it will be one hundred years since De Stijl was founded. We are very grateful to the many people who have contributed to the creation of this book. We are especially indebted to the Chief Government Architect of the Netherlands, Floris Alkemade, for agreeing to write the foreword, and to André Mol of the Office of the Government Architect who advised him in this. In particular we would like to mention here Victor Veldhuijzen van Zanten and Kick van der Pol for their enterprising approach. They proved to be valuable conversational partners. Victor was prepared to contribute ideas to the organization of the publication and provided commentary on a few chapters. Michael White, Ton Idsinga, Nico Nelissen and Els Brinkman also provided useful feedback on a few chapters. In addition, very warm thanks to all those who, during the research for this book, were willing to share their knowledge and opinions in interviews or correspondence: Wies van Moorsel; Maurits de Hoog, EFL Stichting; Wessel de Jonge, TU Delft; Maarten Kloos, former director of Arcam; Reyn van der Lugt, Dutch Drawing Centre foundation; the committee of the Stichting Realisatie Maison d'Artiste; and Anouk de Wit, Van Eesterenmuseum.
For providing quotations about the design's current significance, we are very grateful to Barry R. Campbell, Sjarel Ex, Hubert-Jan Henket, Marieke Kuipers, Wies van Moorsel, K. Schippers and Marek Wieczorek. Many people and institutions helped with the supply of illustrations. It is not possible to name them individually, but we would at least like to thank EFL stichting; Mick Eekhout; Het Nieuwe Instituut Rotterdam; RKD Netherlands Institute for Art History, The Hague; Van Abbemuseum Eindhoven; Centraal Museum Utrecht and the Rietveld-Schröder Archive; Gemeentemuseum Den Haag; and Fondation Custodia Paris. Finally, as compiler and editor, I would like to thank the authors for their contribution and the team from the publishers, who have supported me in this book, in which the architectural history and current relevance of the design are combined: Eelco van Welie, head and heart of nai010 publishers, Brecht Bleeker who kept everything running smoothly along the right track, Robyn de Jong-Dalziel, Maaike Post, Arjen Mulder and Walter van der Star, who diligently translated the texts, and Els Brinkman, who assiduously dotted all the i's. The designer, Lex Reitsma, succeeded in presenting text and image in such a way that Maison d'Artiste is once again able to inspire and contribute to today's culture.

# Credits

This publication was made possible by financial support from the Prins Bernard Cultuurfonds / Ted Schutten Fonds, the Van Eesteren-Fluck & Van Lohuizen Stichting, the Stichting Bevordering van Volkskracht, the Harten Fonds and the De Gijselaar-Hintzenfonds.

Editor
Dolf Broekhuizen
Texts
Ole Bouman, Dolf Broekhuizen, Paul Meurs, Alied Ottevanger, Kees Somer, Wouter Jan Verheul, Michael White
Copy editing
Robyn de Jong-Dalziel
Translation
Robyn de Jong-Dalziel (except essay Michael White), Walter van der Star (French quotes essay Alied Ottenvanger)
Picture editing
Dolf Broekhuizen
with Ingrid Oosterheerd
Graphic design en lithography
Lex Reitsma
Print and binding
Wilco Art Books, Amersfoort
Production
Brecht Bleeker
Publisher
nai010 publishers

PRINS BERNHARD CULTUURFONDS Ted Schutten Fonds

EFL STICHTING

J.E. Jurriaanse Stichting

Harten Fonds

De Gijselaar-Hintzenfonds



nai010 publishers is an internationally orientated publisher specialized in developing, producing and distributing books in the fields of architecture, urbanism, art and design.
www.nai010.com

nai010 books are available internationally at selected bookstores and from the following distribution partners:

North, Central and South America – Artbook | D.A.P., New York, USA, dap@dapinc.com

Rest of the world – Idea Books, Amsterdam, the Netherlands, idea@ideabooks.nl

For general questions, please contact nai010 publishers directly at sales@nai010.com or visit our website www.nai010.com for further information.

Printed and bound in the Netherlands

ISBN 978-94-6208-304-2